STAR WARS

THE MARVEL COVERS

Editor: JEFF YOUNGQUIST
Assistant Editor: SARAH BRUNSTAD
Assistant Managing Editor: JOE HOCHSTEIN
Associate Managing Editor: ALEX STARBUCK
Editors, Special Projects: JENNIFER GRÜNWALD & MARK D. BEAZLEY
SVP Print, Sales & Marketing: DAVID GABRIEL

Editor In Chief: AXEL ALONSO
Chief Creative Officer: JOE QUESADA
Publisher: DAN BUCKLEY

Special thanks to JENNIFER HEDDLE, FRANK PARISI,
JACQUE PORTE, TONY MURPHY & JOSIE HARROLD

STAR WARS

THE MARVEL COVERS

WRITTEN BY
JESS HARROLD

INTRODUCTION BY
AXEL ALONSO

BOOK DESIGN BY
ADAM DEL RE

COVER ART BY
ALEX ROSS

VARIANT COVER ART BY
**JOE QUESADA,
MARK MORALES
& LAURA MARTIN**

Want to see a group of comics professionals at the top of their field tap into their inner child? Take them to the Skywalker Ranch, home of the *Star Wars* archive. I made the pilgrimage back in January 2014 with Jason Aaron, John Cassaday, Kieron Gillen, C.B. Cebulski, and Jordan D. White, shortly after our first meeting with the Lucasfilm Story Group, and it was a game-changing moment for all of us. Surrounded by posters, sketches, props, and costumes that spanned almost 40 years of cinematic history, each of us could not help but reflect on how this unique mythology resonated in our own lives, and the great power and responsibility that comes with shaping it.

Apparently, the trip paid off. Thirty-eight years ago, Marvel Comics released *Star Wars #1*, a movie adaptation published two months before *Star Wars* the movie lit up the silver screen, embarking on what would be a celebrated nine-year run. Last January, we unveiled *Star Wars #1*, the first of several ongoing series that are nothing short of essential reading for any fan of *Star Wars*, and it became the highest-selling comic in more than 20 years: more than a million copies sold and counting. The subsequent success of *Darth Vader, Princess Leia*, and *Kanan: The Last Padawan* proves this was no fluke, and underscores the unique alchemy of *Star Wars* and Marvel Comics. A ripe mythology that resonates across generations, an endless catalog of fascinating characters, and the top creators in comics lining up for an opportunity to play in a sandbox that means so much to so many—was there ever a better recipe for captivating an audience?

To the future.

Axel Alonso

Axel Alonso
Editor in Chief
Marvel Comics

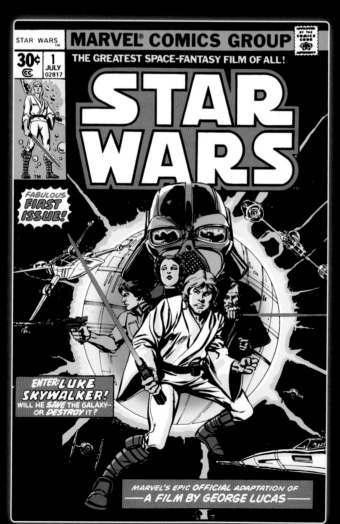

Star Wars (1977) #1
by Howard Chaykin

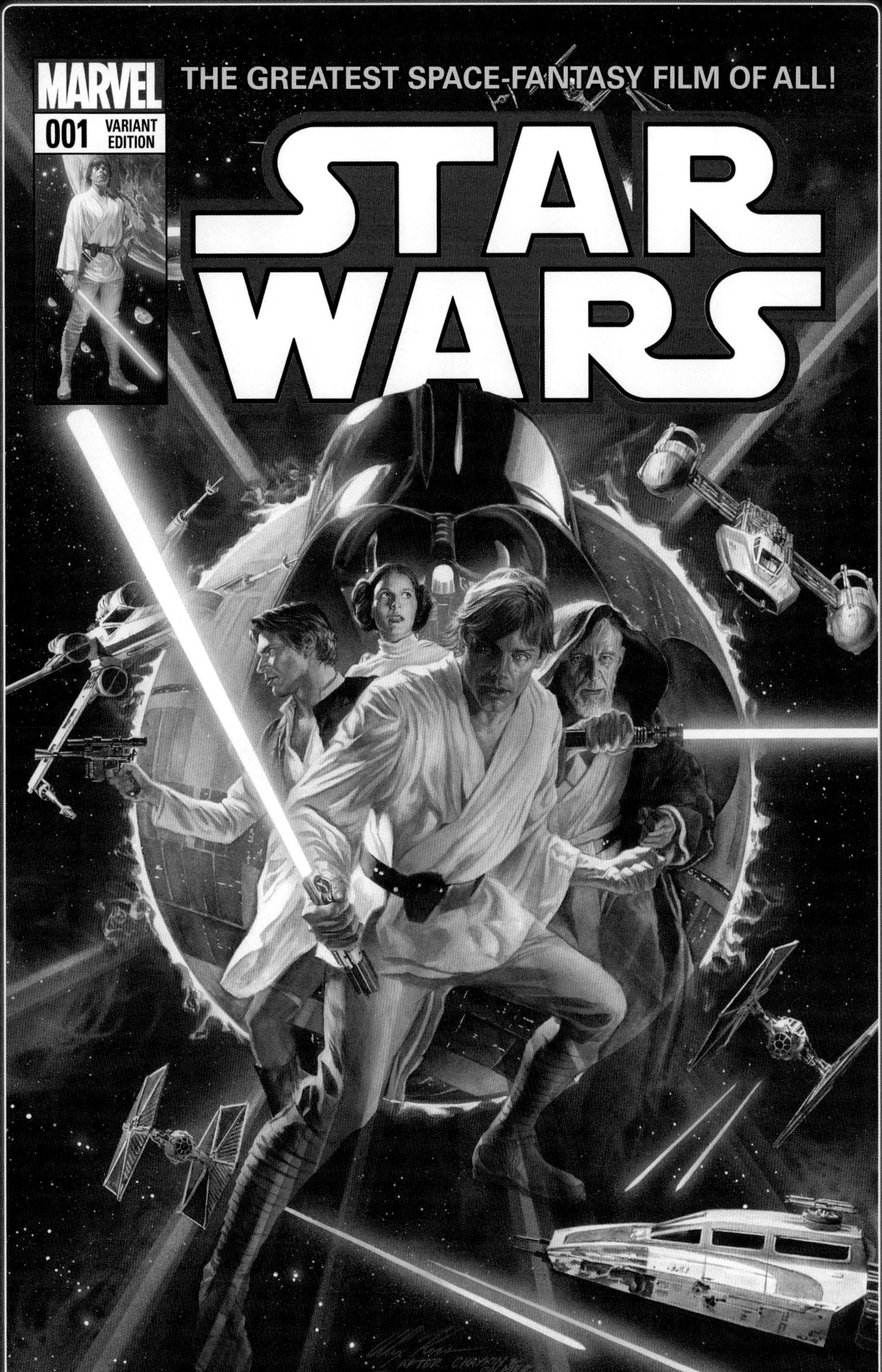
MARVEL
THE GREATEST SPACE-FANTASY FILM OF ALL!
001 VARIANT EDITION
STAR WARS
AFTER CHAYKIN & PALMER

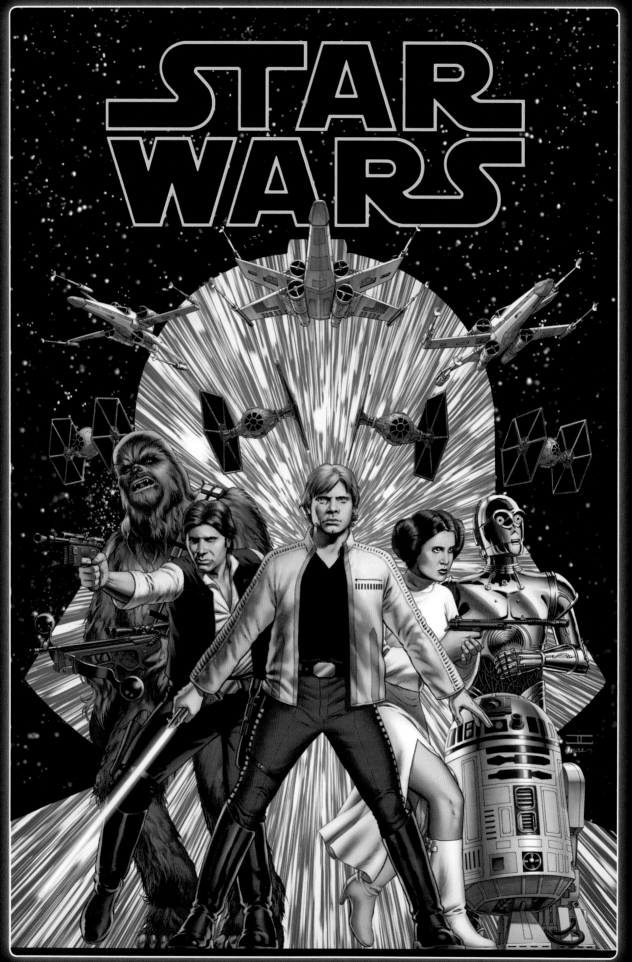

Star Wars #1 Cassaday 2nd Printing Variant—by John Cassaday, colors by Laura Martin

THE FORCE IS STRONG WITH THIS #1

Call it a return, an awakening...a new hope. On January 14, 2015, the first issue of an ongoing *Star Wars* series made its debut—and everything changed. Set immediately after the thrilling climax to *Star Wars Episode IV A New Hope*, *Star Wars #1* ushered in a new beginning for *Star Wars* storytelling, promising original adventures starring Luke Skywalker and his fellow rebels locked in combat with Darth Vader and the Empire. But the book was also a welcome return for an old friend, with the property coming back to Marvel after almost three decades away. And the House of Ideas celebrated in style. Already blessed with the stellar artwork of John Cassaday and the pitch-perfect writing of Jason Aaron, *Star Wars #1* boasted 70 separate covers in its first printing—the 69 collected in this opening chapter plus a blank cover for fans to have customized by their favorite artists. The covers featured work from a who's who of comic-book creators—industry superstars such as Alex Ross and Joe Quesada, veterans of the stature of Alan Davis and Bob McLeod, Marvel stalwarts including Adi Granov and Skottie Young, rising stars such as Sara Pichelli and John Tyler Christopher, and such widely diverse illustrators as Gabriele Dell'Otto and Stan Sakai. And each and every one helped *Star Wars #1* shatter even the publisher's high expectations by becoming the first American comic book in over 20 years to sell more than a million copies.

But the fanfare was not limited to *Star Wars #1*. Quickly joining the flagship series were *Darth Vader* and *Princess Leia*—also featuring top-tier creative teams, with Kieron Gillen and Salvador Larroca on *Vader*, and Mark Waid and Terry Dodson on *Leia*. Those galaxy-expanding titles and subsequent *Star Wars* issues raced to the top of sales charts month after month as excitement spread.

Without doubt, though, none of this success would have been possible without the army of retailers across the world who helped spread the word about *Star Wars* coming back to Marvel—and delivered copy after copy of that landmark first issue into the hands of eager fans. They ordered and sold unprecedented numbers, hosted launch events, and—in several cases—even secured their own exclusive variant covers. Ahead of the gallery of *Star Wars #1* covers that begins this artistic commemoration of a bold new era for *Star Wars* and Marvel, we'd like to salute those on the front line who made it all possible. We're giving the first word to those who so often have the last word on a title's success or failure: the comic-book stores.

"WOW! Everyone's favorite galaxy from far, far away is now back, and everyone just loves it! Our most popular buyers are the older generation buying the comics for the kids or grandkids, and passing the love of *Star Wars* to a new generation! Every week, Marvel delivers a new *Star Wars* comic to eager buyers!"—Drew Lujan, Wantedcomix, Gardena, California

"It's been a fantastic relaunch of the brand, and it's really driven excitement as we approach the new movies. Fans were cautious at first—but when they read the stories, they were pretty pleased and really dove into the new stories. The Alex Ross covers, the J. Scott Campbell covers, and the John Tyler Christopher covers were by far the most successful variants."—Pete Kilmer, Downtown Comics, Indianapolis, Indiana

"Marvel's relaunch of *Star Wars* and the spinoff comics have turned into megahits with my customers. With both great story and art, these comics can't miss. Coupled with the anticipation and buzz of the fans for the next movie, I look forward to Marvel's upcoming plans—timing is everything!"—Rich Brindisi, owner, Comics Express, Floral Park, New York

"The premiere of *Star Wars* at Mile High Comics has been the equivalent of an entirely new comics company entering the scene! As a direct result of this new surge in fan interest, our combined monthly sales of *Star Wars* titles now exceed all the other comics companies in existence, except for the mainstream Marvel and DC super-hero lines. If the Marvel *Star Wars* titles constituted a standalone company, we could easily envision them taking the leadership of the entire comics market after *The Force Awakens* is released. Our favorite cover has to be the Mile High Comics variant edition of *Princess Leia #1*, featuring a stunning cantina image by classically trained Italian artist Gabriele Dell'Otto. That cover has drawn rave reviews and proven to be exceptionally popular with collectors of special limited editions."—Chuck Rozanski, owner, Mile High Comics, Denver, Colorado

"*Star Wars #1* was better received than we could have hoped. We already had quite a few *Star Wars* subscribers, but we more than doubled our *Star Wars* pull list. At Wild Things, the second-print copies of *Star Wars #1* were especially well-received. The classic star-laden cosmic background really spoke to both the nostalgia and the future of the universe for subscribers new and old."—Jeramy Bray, manager, Wild Things Games & Comics, Salem, Oregon

"I grew up a *Star Wars* fan. My very first experience with the classic tale wasn't with the movie—it was with the Marvel Comics adaptation of the first movie. The original Marvel run is some of my fondest memories of early childhood reading because not only did it give me more *Star Wars*, but it also expanded on the wonderful universe created by George Lucas. From the ComicXposure variant to the homage covers, there were so many great variants for *Star Wars #1*, but my favorite has to be the Alex Ross homage to the original *Star Wars #1* from 1977. The image alone takes me right back to my childhood and fills me with nostalgic memories. I am so excited about the next movie installment coming this Christmas and to see what the expanding *Star Wars* universe has in store for us in the comics. Fan support for the series has been astounding—and as a fan myself, I can say with all confidence the *Star Wars* brand is right back where it has always belonged: with the House of Ideas."—Michael Breakfield, Lone Star Comics, Arlington, Texas

John Cassaday's *Star Wars #1* cover was so successful it received colorful new printings.

SEARCH YOUR FEELINGS
What the critics said about *Star Wars #1*

"This first issue feels like a reunion with some long-absent friends."
—David Pepose, *Newsarama*

"After all of the hype, and talk of it being the best-selling comic of the new millennium,
it was going to be hard for *Star Wars #1* to live up to expectations. These expectations
were not only met, but exceeded to the point where I'm reminded why I love
this fictional universe like I do."
—John Ernenputsch, *Comicosity*

"*Star Wars #1* simply feels like a true *Star Wars* story. Jason Aaron, John Cassaday,
and Laura Martin nail it completely. When you open the comic, and see and read those
first few pages, you'll likely hear the familiar theme song playing in your head...
This is exactly the *Star Wars* comic I was hoping for."
—Tony "G-Man" Guerrero, *Comic Vine*

"*Star Wars #1* is the perfect *Star Wars* comic. It captures the tone and feel of the films,
while beginning a story that fits seamlessly into the beloved universe."
—Chase Magnett, *ComicBook.com*

"*Star Wars #1* is a fitting and superbly constructed homecoming, one that is inviting to more
casual fans while delivering excellent storytelling that will encourage existing fans to make
the jump to lightspeed and travel to the franchise's once and future home."
—Jim Johnson, *Comic Book Resources*

"At times it feels like watching an unreleased *Star Wars* movie, and that's magic well worth the five bucks."
—Joshua Yehl, *IGN*

"Jason Aaron and John Cassaday are up to the challenge. They are able to turn their fond love
for these characters into something more: an expertly paced reintroduction to some old friends.
From the opening scroll to the first reveal of those familiar heroes, everything about the
book screams *Star Wars*. It's like we never left that galaxy far, far away."
—Pierce Lydon, *Newsarama*

NEVER TELL ME THE ODDS!

The many *Star Wars #1* variants span the width and breadth of the long-ago, faraway galaxy—from household names like Luke Skywalker and the crew of the *Millennium Falcon* to beloved supporting players like Lando Calrissian and the Ewoks to less instantly memorable faces like Greedo, Ponda Baba, and other patrons of the Mos Eisley cantina. But which characters are most likely to feature on the many *Star Wars #1* covers that follow? Taking each individual illustration into account once—no double-counting for black-and-white variants—makes a total of 47 possible appearances, and the following figures are all represented at least twice. The roll call may not surprise you—but the precise order just might!

LUKE SKYWALKER 28 covers (60%)

HAN SOLO 27 covers (57%)

PRINCESS LEIA 22 covers (47%)

DARTH VADER 21 covers (45%)

CHEWBACCA 18 covers (38%)

C-3PO 11 covers (23%)

R2-D2 11 covers (23%)

BOBA FETT 11 covers (23%)

STORMTROOPERS 10 covers (21%)

OBI-WAN KENOBI 4 covers (9%)

EMPEROR PALPATINE 4 covers (9%)

YODA 3 covers (6%)

JABBA THE HUTT 2 covers (4%)

YOU CANNOT ESCAPE YOUR DESTINY

John Cassaday was fated to someday, somehow, draw *Star Wars*. First and foremost, as writer Jason Aaron puts it, Cassaday is "the world's biggest *Star Wars* fan." Recounting the Marvel creators' visit to the Skywalker Ranch, during which they enjoyed a tour of the Lucasfilm archives, Aaron says, "Nobody was a bigger *Star Wars* geek than Cassaday. He seemed to recognize more of the blasters, lightsabers, and ships than anybody else. He was definitely geeking out."

Second, the artist has earned a reputation for bringing cinematic scope to the printed page on his many critically acclaimed projects, from *Planetary* for DC Comics' Wildstorm imprint to his blockbuster collaboration with writer Joss Whedon on Marvel's *Astonishing X-Men*.

So who better to bring the sheer excitement and sense of wonder of the beloved film series to all-new comic-book adventures?

"We knew it was going to be considered canon, and there's a great weight that goes along with that," Cassaday says. "Lucasfilm was going to be heavily involved as consultants and overall gatekeepers." Describing his time at the Skywalker Ranch in March 2014, Cassaday continues, "We discussed story outlines, character approaches, and basic design ideas for what was coming. There was a lot to take in, but half my homework was done, considering I'd been eating up these stories since I was five years old."

know the shot and expression, and can fit the likeness in just right, but I don't want to be pigeonholed into that commitment at the expense of the moment. The story and the character always come first."

Almost four decades later, Cassaday translated that lifetime of buildup into some of the finest work of an already impressive career. His secret? Stick to what works. "The key for me with *Star Wars* is to stay in their world," he explains. "Don't get in the way of what is already known. I think of the basic nature of the filmmaking process that worked so well for the original trilogy. No stylistic flights of fancy for the sake of showing off. Tell the story, get the shot, get the performances, and move on." That approach influences his own take on the iconic cast at his disposal as he delivers perfectly realized characters that are both instantly recognizable yet unmistakably Cassaday. "My perspective from the beginning was to consider the character, the actor, and my stylistic tendencies, and throw them into a blender—and what comes out is what comes out," he says. "There are times where I

Two of those characters in particular stand out for the artist: "I've loved all these characters most of my life, but I gotta say that Han Solo proved to be even more fun than I'd anticipated. Harrison Ford's face just has so much character to play with. He's such an eye-rolling, crooked-grinned rollercoaster of badassism. Vader is interesting in the opposite way. While he's a stoic robot design without facial expression, the audience can read into his emotions because they know the character. With Jason's spot-on dialogue, they can hear the voice and understand what's under the helmet. My job is half done before I even start drawing."

or possibly a puppet. If they couldn't do it then, I won't do it now." And in achieving that aim of making his series work convincingly as a virtual Episode IV-and-a-half, Cassaday extends praise to colorist Laura Martin for helping keep the approach "basic and filmic." He adds, "The movies wisely never stretch too far with cinematography tricks, so neither should we. Laura and I have worked together many times over, and she certainly knows the *Star Wars* universe. So it was a natural fit, and she's doing a fantastic job."

Clearly, Cassaday has poured his heart and soul into every page, and he hopes those who buy his issues will share his excitement. "Honestly, I just want the reader to turn on the John Williams music as they crack the sucker open," he says. "From there on, if we've done our job, I think they'll find themselves immersed in a stellar experience from long ago and far away. I know I have."

Cassaday's insistence on authenticity also extends to his own original contributions to the book—and, in turn, to the *Star Wars* mythos. "From the start, I knew my approach to the overall design on the book would be very much in touch with the practical filmmaking of the original trilogy," he expands. "I wanted to embrace the limitations of technology, makeup, and costuming from that era—no intricate, over-the-top CGI or mocap. So when I design an alien figure, I keep in mind that it's an actor wearing a rubber mask or prosthetics,

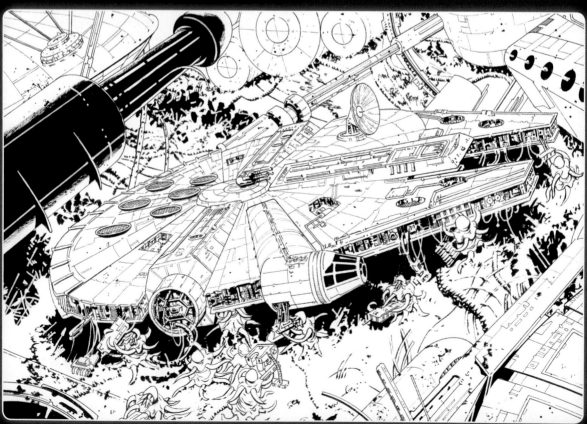

"The Force is strong
with this one."

Star Wars #1 Cassaday Premiere Variant—by John Cassaday, colors by Laura Martin

Star Wars #1—pencils and inks by John Cassaday, colors by Laura Martin

Star Wars #1 Quesada Variant

pencils by Joe Quesada, inks by Mark Morales, colors by Laura Martin

Star Wars #1 Quesada Sketch Variant

pencils by Joe Quesada, inks by Mark Morales

Star Wars #1 Acuña Heroes & Fantasies Black and White Variant—by Daniel Acuña

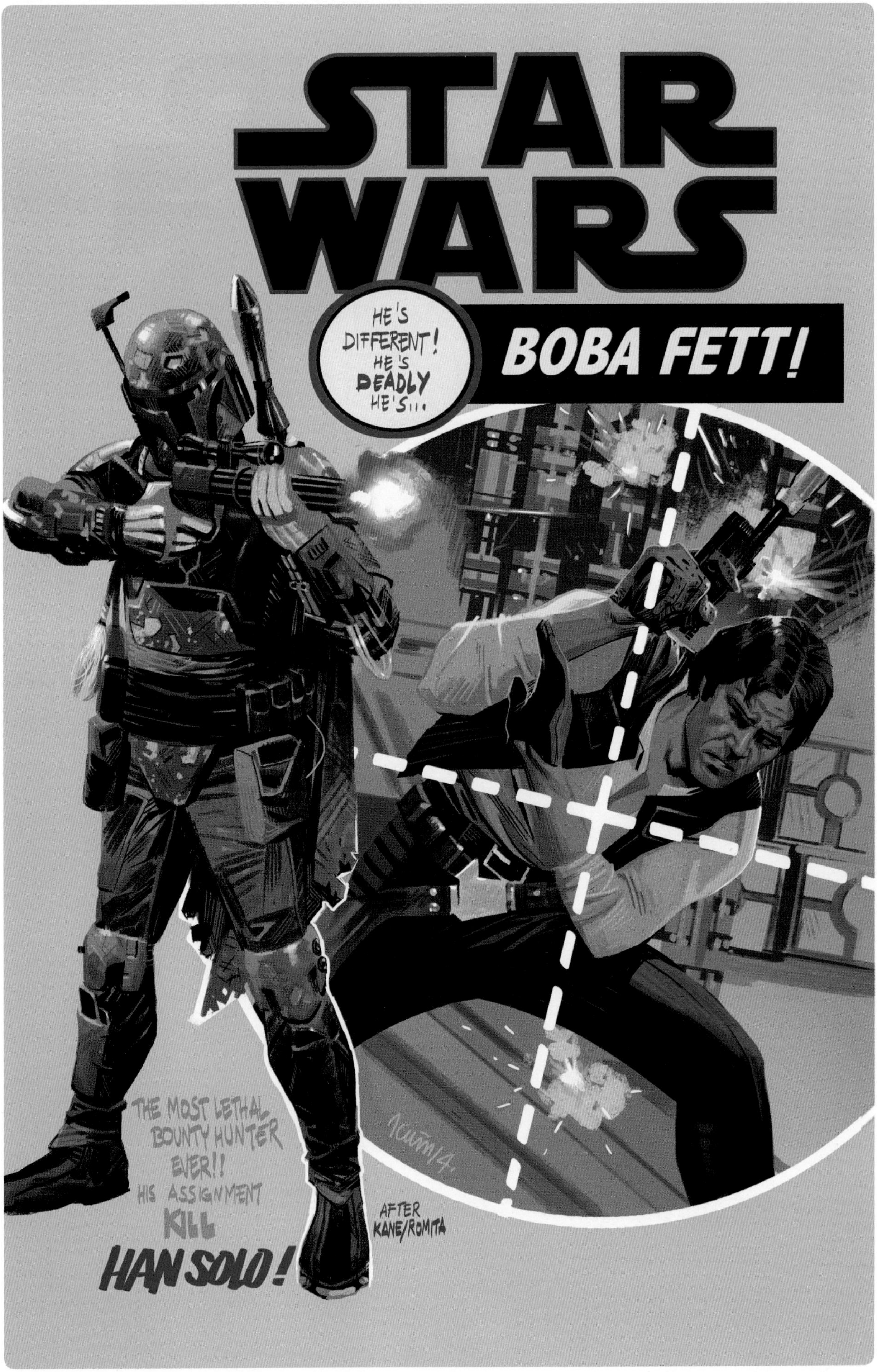
STAR WARS
HE'S DIFFERENT! HE'S DEADLY HE'S...
BOBA FETT!
THE MOST LETHAL BOUNTY HUNTER EVER!! HIS ASSIGNMENT KILL HAN SOLO!
AFTER KANE/ROMITA
Acuña/14.

Star Wars #1 Acuña Heroes & Fantasies Variant—by Daniel Acuña

Star Wars #1 Movie Variant

Star Wars #1 Bianchi Bam Variant—by Simone Bianchi

Star Wars #1 Brooks Midtown Black and White Variant—by Mark Brooks

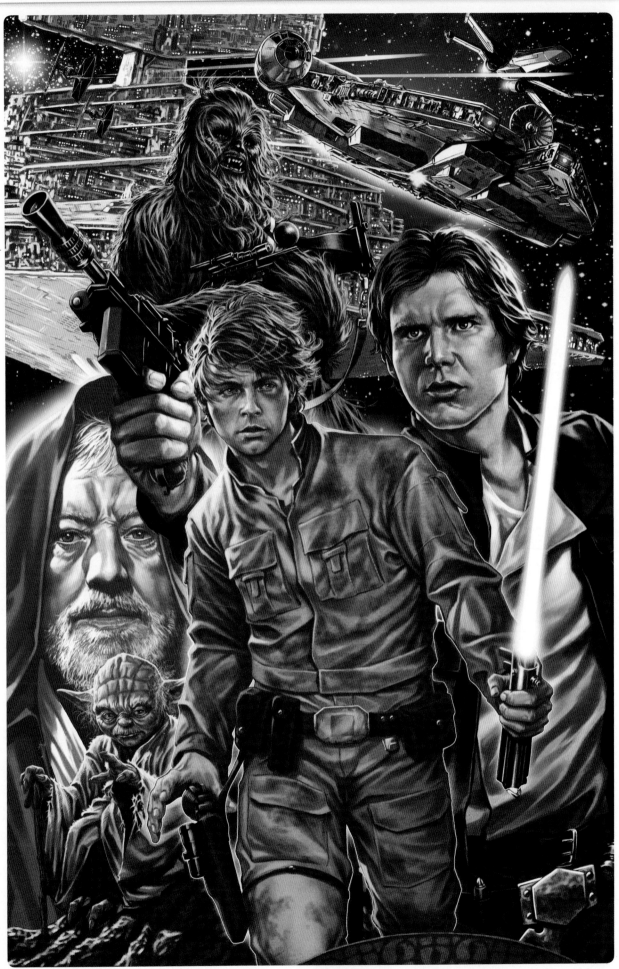

Star Wars #1 Brooks Midtown Variant—by Mark Brooks

Darth Vader #1, *Star Wars #1*, and *Princess Leia #1*
Brooks Midtown Black and White
Variants—by Mark Brooks

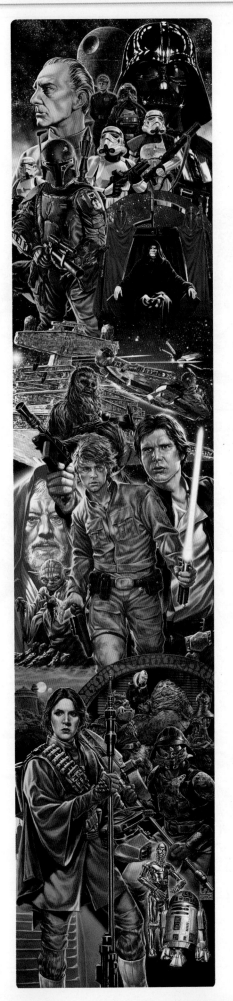

Darth Vader #1, Star Wars #1, and *Princess Leia #1*
Brooks Midtown Variants—by Mark Brooks

Star Wars #1 Campbell Cargo Hold Black and White Variant—by J. Scott Campbell

Star Wars #1 Campbell Cargo Hold Variant—pencils and inks by J. Scott Campbell, colors by Nei Ruffino

Star Wars #1 Campbell Industry G Black and White Variant—by J. Scott Campbell

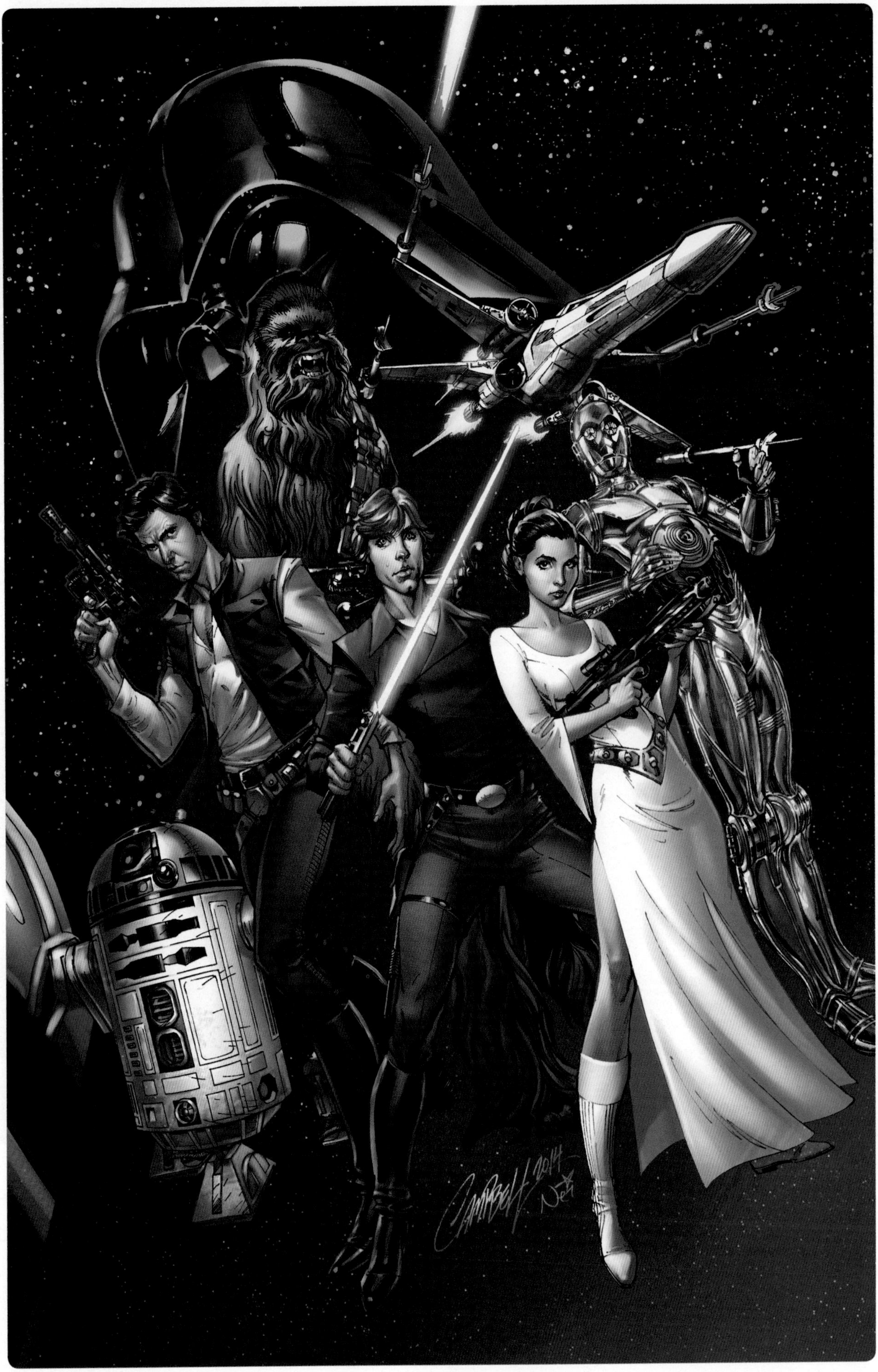
CAMPBELL 2014
Nei

Star Wars #1 Campbell Connecting Variant—pencils and inks by J. Scott Campbell, colors by Nei Ruffino

Darth Vader #1, *Star Wars #1*, and *Princess Leia #1* Campbell Connecting Variants

pencils and inks by J. Scott Campbell, colors by Nei Ruffino

Star Wars #1 Campion Comic Kings Variant—by Pascal Campion

Star Wars #1 Cho Comics, Cards & Collectibles Variant—pencils and inks by Frank Cho, colors by Jason Keith

Star Wars #1 Christopher ComicXposure Black and White Variant—by John Tyler Christopher

Star Wars #1 Christopher ComicXposure Variant—by John Tyler Christopher

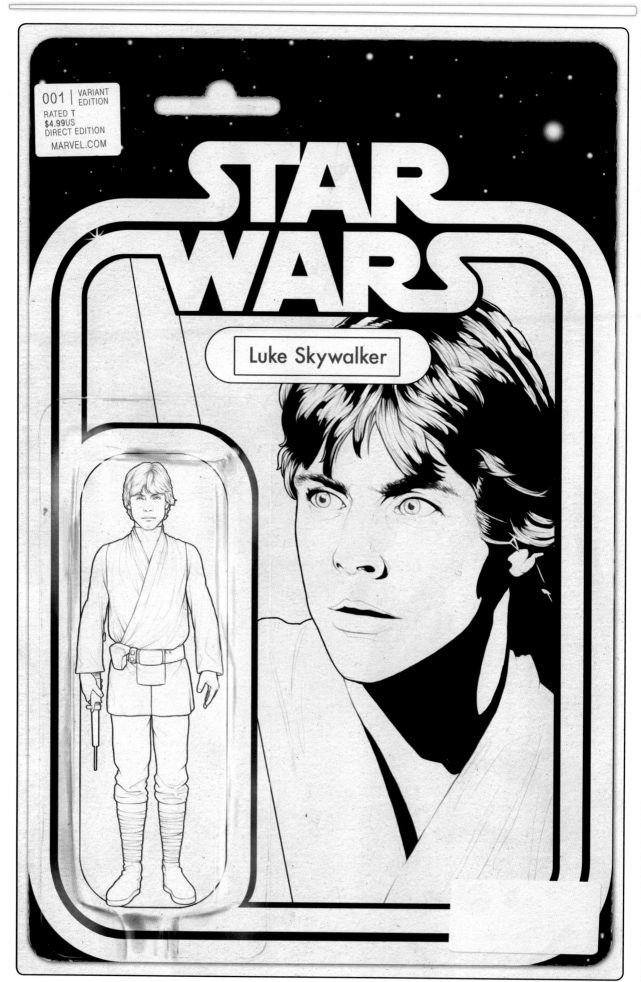

Star Wars #1 Christopher DCD Breakfast Variant—by John Tyler Christopher

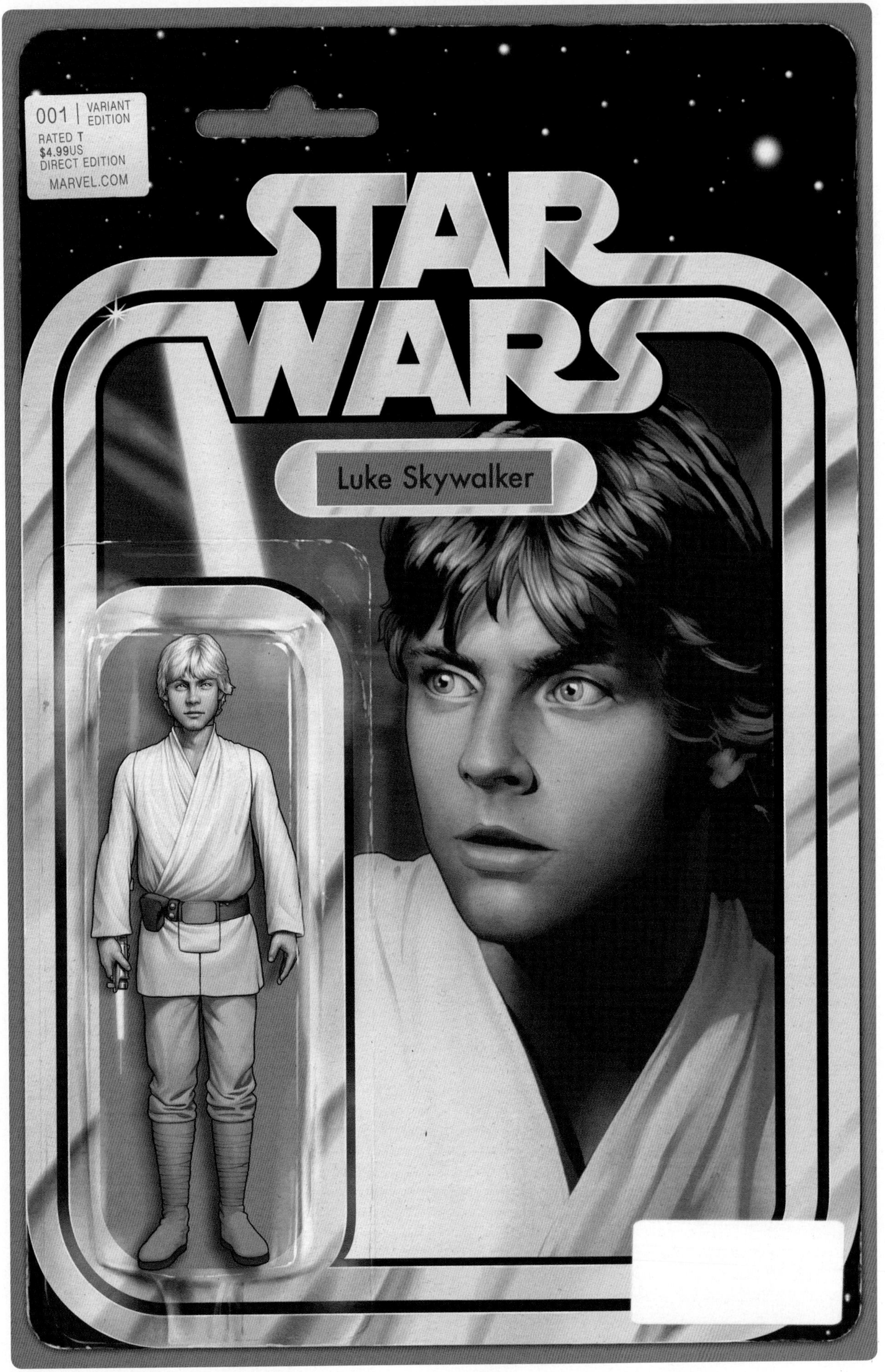

<image_block type="text_on_image">
001 | VARIANT
EDITION
RATED T
$4.99US
DIRECT EDITION
MARVEL.COM

STAR
WARS

Luke Skywalker
</image_block>

Star Wars #1 Christopher Action Figure Variant—by John Tyler Christopher

I HAVE A BAD FEELING ABOUT THIS...

That was little John Tyler Christopher's reaction when he saw Michael Jackson's "Thriller" video for the first time. Luckily, the boy who would one day grow up to be a successful comic-book artist had an unconventional guardian to protect him. "Thriller scared me to death," he recalls. "It was the scariest thing I ever saw—and, in my mind, the only thing that could protect me from the dancing zombie-werecat Michael Jackson was the rancor. I literally slept with the rancor as my teddy bear for four or five months."

Fast-forward three decades, and he had a "bad feeling" once again when he first got the call about a new project to add to what he describes as his already "insane" schedule. But then he heard the details, and it was an offer he couldn't refuse—a series of variant covers, each one designed to look like a classic Kenner *Star Wars* action figure. This was a project Christopher was born to draw. "I don't remember a time in my life without *Star Wars*," he says. "It's a huge part of my life, it really is.

"I would argue that *Star Wars* is one of the top-five most important films of all time, not just for what it did for science fiction and that genre—it created the idea of the blockbuster. It changed the way people market and advertise and make movies. George Lucas was a genius when it came to things like this. We would not have *Marvel's The Avengers* without *Star Wars*—it led the charge with the idea of the merchandise and the marketing and all that stuff becoming so integral to how not even just movies, but entertainment itself was handled. It's massive."

And for Christopher, not only were action figures a fundamental part of *Star Wars'* success, but the films also changed the toy market in return. "I think they go hand-in-hand," he says. "It was, for me, the first toy that I ever collected. *Star Wars* didn't create the action figure, but I believe it popularized it. It wasn't just the one character. There were, like, 30 action figures in the original line." In fact, 33 figures in total were released in the wake of *A New Hope*, including a Boba Fett that could only be obtained by mailing away proofs of purchase from the other toys. "You know you had to collect them all," Christopher enthuses. "It was a big thing. Me and my cousin would collect them, and we'd each have to get Vader, obviously, and Boba Fett, but because we didn't have enough money for all of them, we were like, 'How about you get this guy, and I'll get this guy, and together we'll have all of them.' We strategized."

That collector's compulsion, he believes, drove his generation's fascination with *Star Wars*, and is a key reason stories continue to be told to this day. "One of the brilliant things of *Star Wars* to me is the idea of 'the universe,' the perception of ownership," he says. "More so than anything else, as a kid, you believe in the entire backstory about Hammerhead and Snaggletooth and half the characters in the Cantina. It's because little kids were sitting out playing with these characters—being like, 'What did that guy do? Why was he in the Cantina?'—acting out beautiful scenes. And as they grow up, they

have a cool idea: Now that I'm a novel writer, I'm a comic-book writer, could they fit into my story? That's how they build a universe. *Star Wars* built a universe that is more substantial than any movies, than most television shows do. It's truly as big as *Star Trek*, and *Star Trek* has, what, six TV series and however many movies? It's astounding, and I think a lot of it has to do with the action figures allowing children to create that galaxy in their head, and eventually share it with the world."

When it came time to squeeze the action-figure variants into his schedule—ultimately more than doubled in number, with the eight so far collected in this volume—Christopher pulled all his old toys out of his parents' loft for reference. He says he "went all-out with the package design"—trying to make sure that while the actual-figure component of his covers was a "representation of reality," the background picture was the "real deal," with more of a photographic look. For him, it's all about evoking an emotional reaction in fans of a similar vintage, and he achieves it with the aid of a special expert: "My personal barometer is, 'What would five-year-old John think?' Because if five-year-old John thinks it's cool, hell yeah, you gotta do it." That's the secret of covers packed with detail, including Easter Eggs for fans who really know their *Star Wars* toys—such as the Luke Skywalker figure on his *Star Wars #1* variant. "I always thought it was really funny that Luke had this neon-yellow hair, so I had to put that in the action figure," he says. "Five-year-old John would think that was really funny. I painstakingly tried to make sure that the hair on the background image was that dirty, sandy brown color to create that juxtaposition—like, 'Look, I know you know Mark Hamill's hair is brown, but the figure was neon-yellow, and that's awesome.'"

With Leia, he made the head a "little squatter" than Carrie Fisher's, because the figure "had a really round head." She's also depicted with the original toy's "pant suit" rather than the dress from the film. Han Solo's head is thinner and longer than Harrison Ford's, while Darth Vader's helmet brought its own challenges. "When I drew the Vader action figure, something looked off. It looked too light, if that makes sense. I realized that the chin in my drawing was a lot higher up than it was in Vader's actual figure. It had a more squat face, and the helmet was a lot thinner. So I actually didn't nail it until I started making these very subtle manipulations to the character."

But one figure was so close to his heart that Christopher himself secured an exclusive on the cover: "I actually bought the rights to do the Boba Fett action figure cover. I think that having that toy as a kid, you just look at him like this guy's amazing. Back then, you couldn't just go buy Boba Fett, you had to earn Boba Fett by buying other characters. He was built up to be this enigma. If you had Boba Fett, it was a badge of honor."

And now the same is true of Christopher's highly sought-after Boba Fett variant—which, naturally, is loaded with nostalgic attention to detail. "He's got a blue helmet as opposed to green," Christopher says. "The shoulder armor is not the same. There's no way, shape, or form—by today's standards—if I was to send that off as my Boba Fett figure design, they'd accept it. They'd be like, 'That's not Boba Fett.' There would be a laundry list of why it was wrong. But the kids back then didn't give a damn, because he looks cool." Other subtle touches include areas where paint has chipped off the figure—to reflect the fact that, in the movies, Boba Fett's armor is "all beat up."

For the artist, this has been one of the best assignments of his career, an "absolute trip down memory lane." At the risk of mixing his sci-fi films, he adds, "Working on this has been the closest thing to buying a DeLorean and traveling back in time to do my job. I'm just reveling in it. It has been like one of the most enjoyable projects I've ever had to privilege of working on." In short—and no doubt to the delight of his rancor-clinging inner five-year-old—Christopher has a good feeling about this.

STAY ON TARGET!
Where to find all the Christopher Action Figure Variants included in this volume...

LUKE SKYWALKER
Star Wars #1—page 39

HAN SOLO
Star Wars #2—page 108

OBI-WAN KENOBI
Star Wars #3—page 111

CHEWBACCA
Star Wars #4—page 120

BOBA FETT
Star Wars #4—page 121

C-3PO
Star Wars #5—page 125

R2-D2
Star Wars #6—page 130

DARTH VADER
Darth Vader #1—page 146

PRINCESS LEIA
Princess Leia #1—page 183

Star Wars #1 Christopher Party Sketch Variant—by John Tyler Christopher

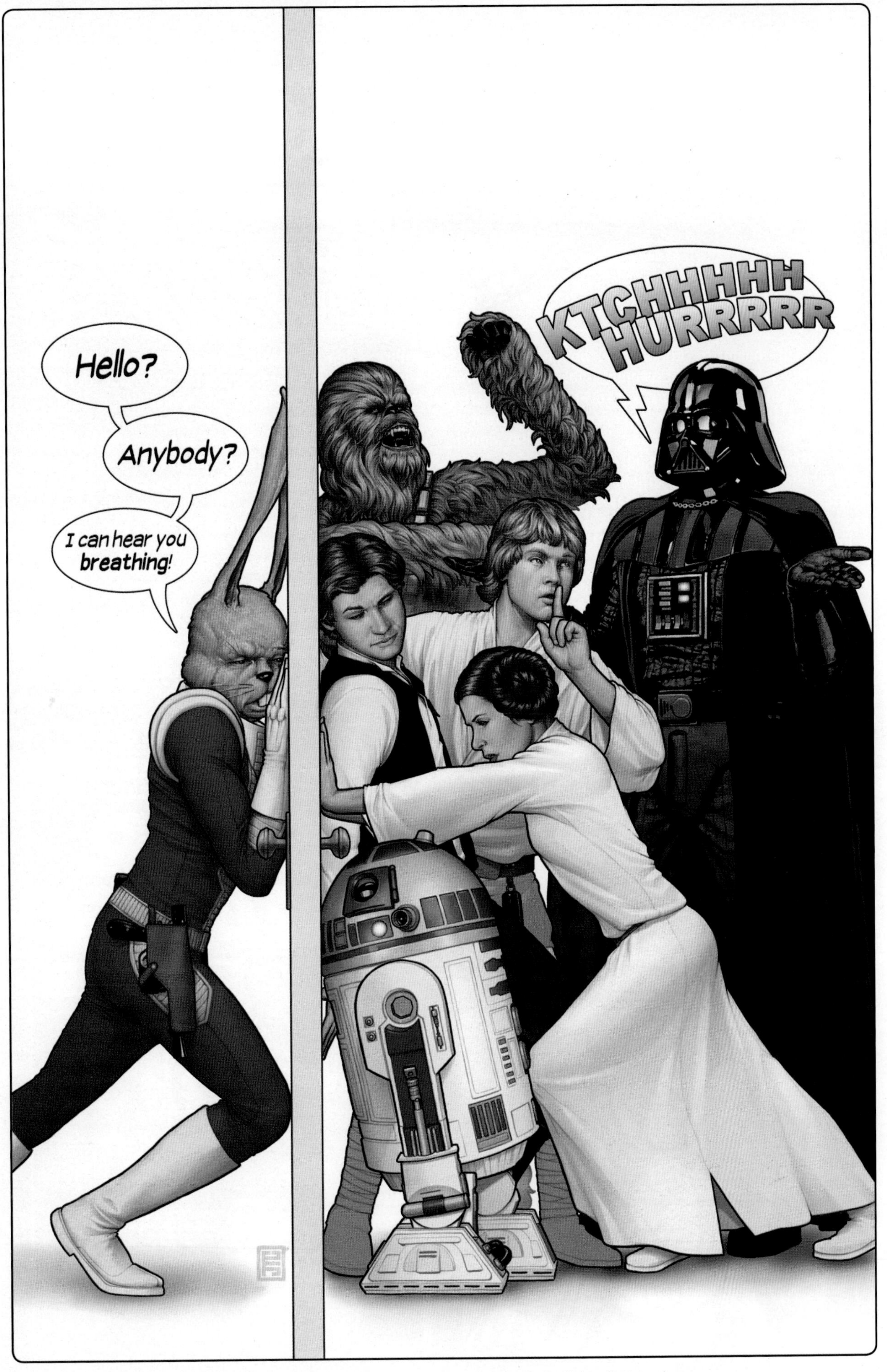
Hello?
Anybody?
I can hear you breathing!
KTCHHHHH HURRRRR

Star Wars #1 Christopher Party Variant—by John Tyler Christopher

LAUGH IT UP, FUZZBALL!

As noted humorist Chewbacca would no doubt confirm, John Tyler Christopher takes the prize for the funniest *Star Wars #1* cover with his Party Variant. But who's the oversized bunny rabbit whose name isn't on the guest list? Why that would be Jaxxon, the smart-talking Lepi smuggler from Coachella Prime who is arguably the most famous original creation of the first Marvel *Star Wars* series.

Introduced by Roy Thomas and Howard Chaykin in *Star Wars #8*, cover-dated February 1978, Jaxxon was recruited by Han Solo and Chewbacca to join their "Eight Against a World!" and made four more appearances in subsequent issues. But while his leporine form ensured he was a memorable addition to the wider *Star Wars* family, he was not universally popular. As Thomas has recounted in his magazine, *Alter Ego*, George Lucas "particularly disliked…a six-foot alien who resembled a green Bugs Bunny in space gear." Thomas wrote, "I had figured my 'green rabbit' Jaxxon wasn't really much weirder than a Wookiee, but obviously George, as the creator of the *Star Wars* mythos, felt differently."

But while Jax, for short (which, he would quickly remind you, he ain't), may have had one high-profile detractor, he left his mark on an impressionable young fan: a boy who grew up to live the dream and put the character back on the front cover of *Star Wars*, if only for one variant. "Jaxxon is awesome," Christopher maintains. "He is cool like a B-movie sci-fi character. Some people dismiss him as a silly comic-book character, but the nature of him is that he's just a six-and-a-half-foot-tall bunny rabbit. It's hard for him not to be silly, but that's the charm of the character. I love that kind of stuff."

As a result, Christopher jumped at the chance to feature Jaxxon on his Party Variant, even if the poor guy ended up the butt of the joke. "That character has not been drawn professionally for, like, 30 years. To have the opportunity to do that and be the only person who had drawn it in that length of time was really exciting for me. Obviously, stylistically, comic art has changed so much in that time, and it was a really cool challenge to do it."

With Jaxxon back in the public eye, courtesy of Christopher, who knows—the character might actually get his lucky rabbit's foot in that door one day.

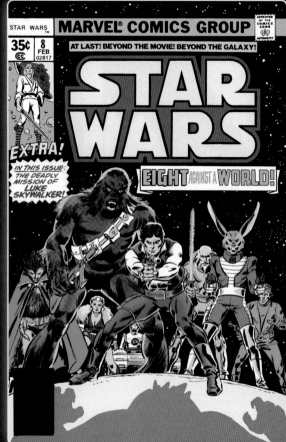

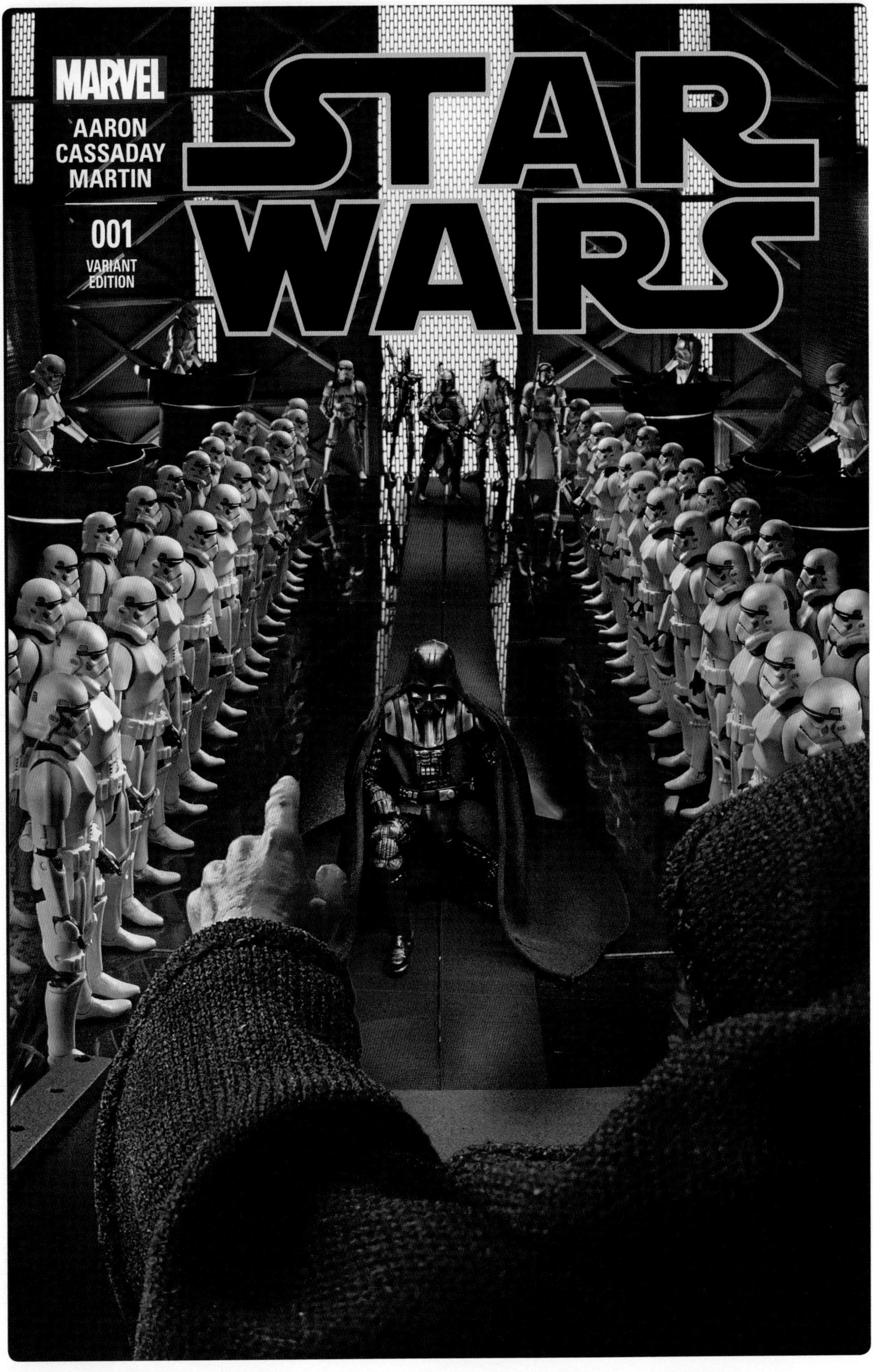
MARVEL
AARON
CASSADAY
MARTIN
001
VARIANT
EDITION
STAR WARS

Star Wars #1 Hasbro Previews Exclusive Variant

Star Wars #1 Conner Vault Collectibles Black and White Variant—by Amanda Conner

Star Wars #1 Conner Vault Collectibles Variant—pencils and inks by Amanda Conner, colors by Paul Mounts

Star Wars #1 Davis Emerald City Comics Black and White Variant—pencils by Alan Davis, inks by Mark Farmer

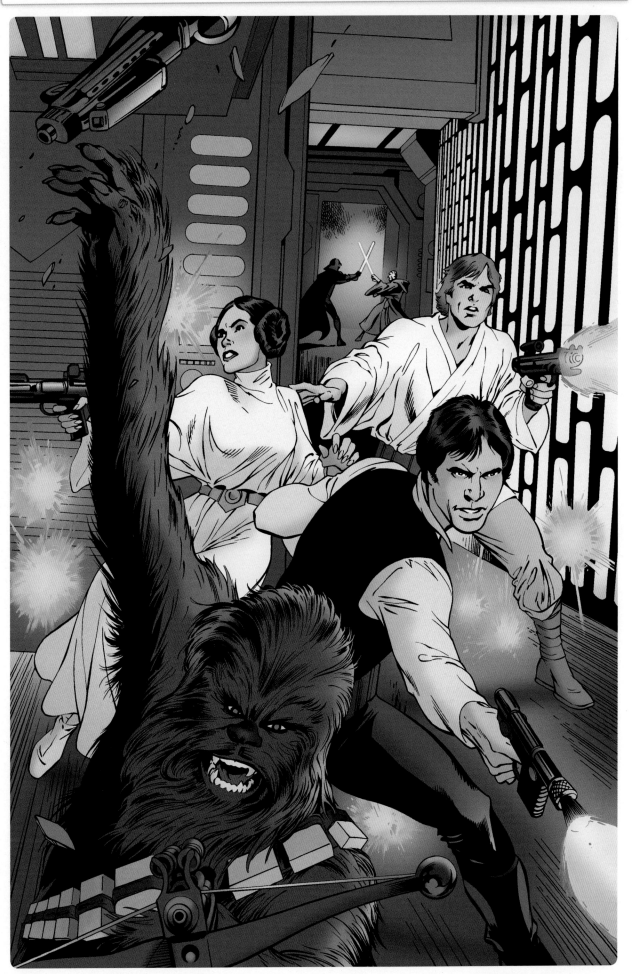

Star Wars #1 Davis Emerald City Comics Variant—pencils by Alan Davis, inks by Mark Farmer, colors by Muntsa Vicente

Star Wars #1 Dell'Otto Loot Crate Variant—by Gabriele Dell'Otto

Star Wars #1 Del Mundo EMP Museum Variant—by Mike Del Mundo

Star Wars #1 Deodato Limited Edition Comix Black and White Variant—by Mike Deodato Jr.

Star Wars #1 Deodato Limited Edition Comix Variant—pencils and inks by Mike Deodato Jr., colors by Frank Martin

Star Wars #1 Dorman M&M Comics Variant—by Dave Dorman

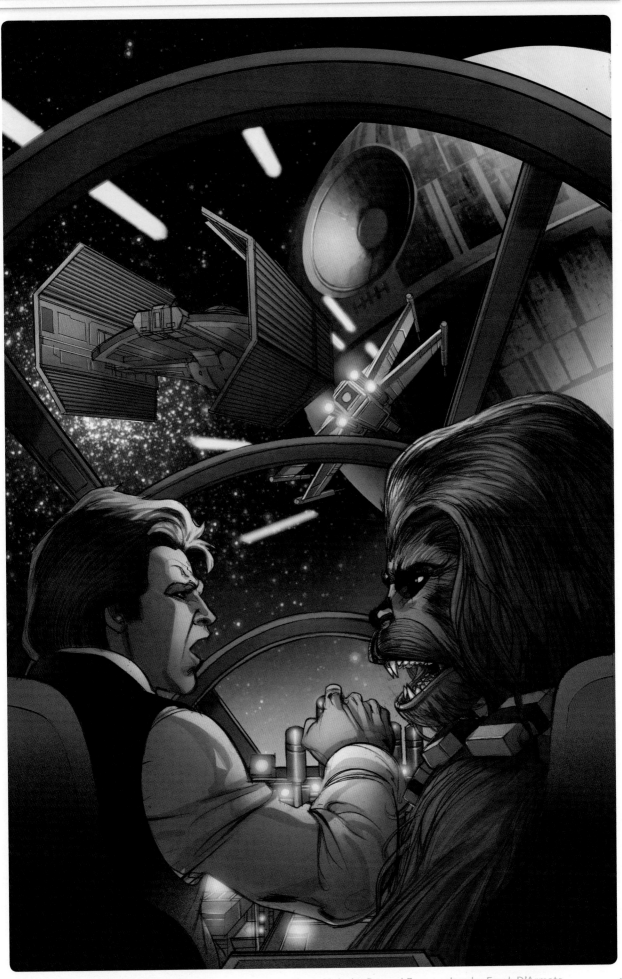

Star Wars #1 Ferry ThinkGeek Variant—pencils and inks by Pasqual Ferry, colors by Frank D'Armata

Star Wars #1 Frison BuyMeToys Variant—by Jenny Frison

Star Wars #1 Hans Rebel Base Comics Variant—by Stephanie Hans

Star Wars #1 Granov Forbidden Planet Black and White Variant—by Adi Granov

Star Wars #1 Granov Forbidden Planet Variant —by Adi Granov

Star Wars #1 Horn GameStop Variant—by Greg Horn

Star Wars #1 Keown Third Eye Comics Variant—enhanced pencils by Dale Keown, colors by Jason Keith

Star Wars #1 Keown AOD Collectables Black and White Variant—by Dale Keown

Star Wars #1 Keown AOD Collectables Variant—enhanced pencils by Dale Keown, colors by Jason Keith

Star Wars #1 Land Dynamite Entertainment Black and White Variant—by Greg Land

Star Wars #1 Land Dynamite Entertainment Variant—pencils and inks by Greg Land, colors by Justin Ponsor

Star Wars #1 Larroca Fan Expo Sketch Fade Variant—pencils and inks by Salvador Larroca, colors by Edgar Delgado

Star Wars #1 Larroca Fan Expo Variant—pencils and inks by Salvador Larroca, colors by Edgar Delgado

Star Wars #1 Maleev DCBS Black and White Variant—by Alex Maleev

Star Wars #1 Maleev DCBS Variant—by Alex Maleev

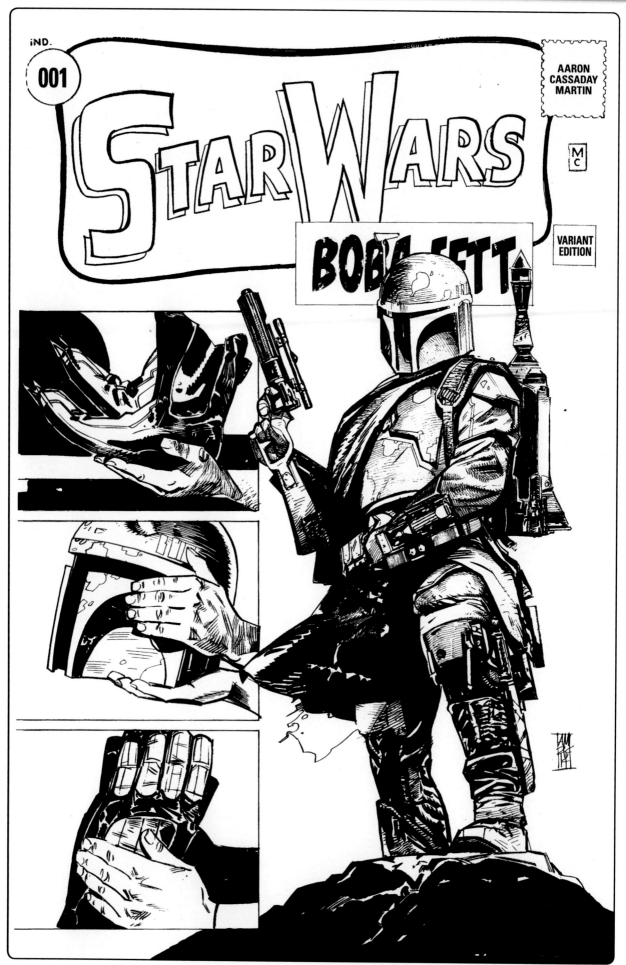

Star Wars #1 Maleev Warp 9 Black and White Variant—by Alex Maleev

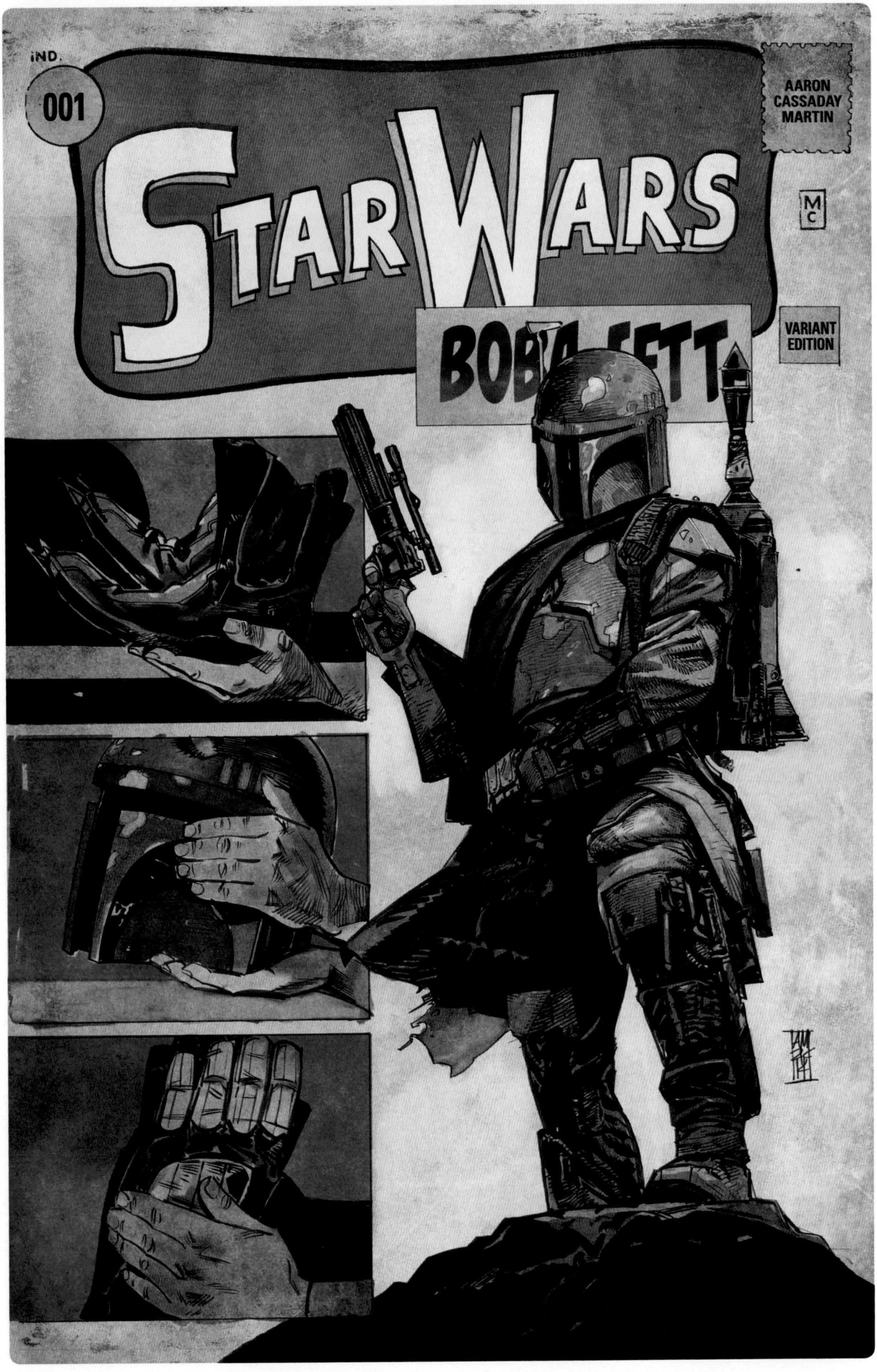

IND.
001
STAR WARS
BOBA FETT
AARON
CASSADAY
MARTIN
MC
VARIANT
EDITION

Star Wars #1 Maleev Warp 9 Variant—by Alex Maleev

Star Wars #1 Mayhew Zapp Comics Black and White Variant—by Mike Mayhew

Star Wars #1 Mayhew Zapp Comics Variant—pencils and inks by Mike Mayhew, colors by Rainier Beredo

Star Wars #1 McKone Bampf Limited Variant—pencils and inks by Mike McKone, colors by Jason Keith

Star Wars #1 McLeod variant—pencils and inks by Bob McLeod, colors by Frank D'Armata

Star Wars #1 Perkins Heroes Haven Comics Variant—pencils and inks by Mike Perkins, colors by Andy Troy

Star Wars #1 Petersen Newbury Comics Variant—by David Petersen

Star Wars #1 Pichelli Variant—pencils and inks by Sara Pichelli, colors by Justin Ponsor

Star Wars #1 Quinones Kings Comics Variant—by Joe Quinones

Star Wars #1 Ramos Mile High Comics Variant—pencils and inks by Humberto Ramos, colors by Edgar Delgado

Star Wars #1 Renaud Fantastico Variant—by Paul Renaud

Star Wars #1 Renaud Hot Topic Variant—by Paul Renaud

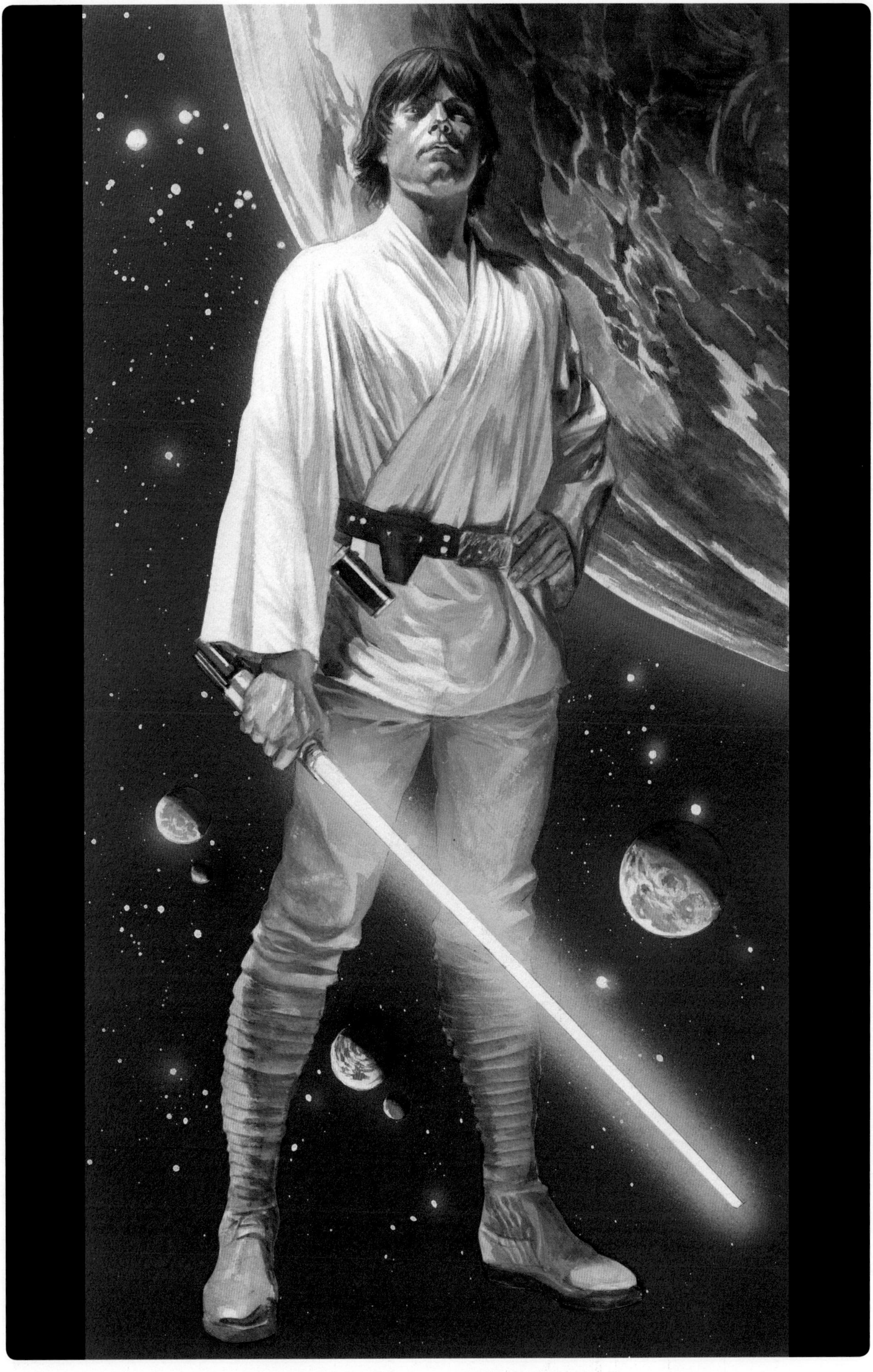

Star Wars #1 AlexRossStore.com Variant—by Alex Ross

Star Wars #1 Ross Sketch Variant—by Alex Ross

Star Wars #1 Ross Variant—by Alex Ross

Star Wars #1 Sakai Corner Store Comics Black and White Variant—by Stan Sakai

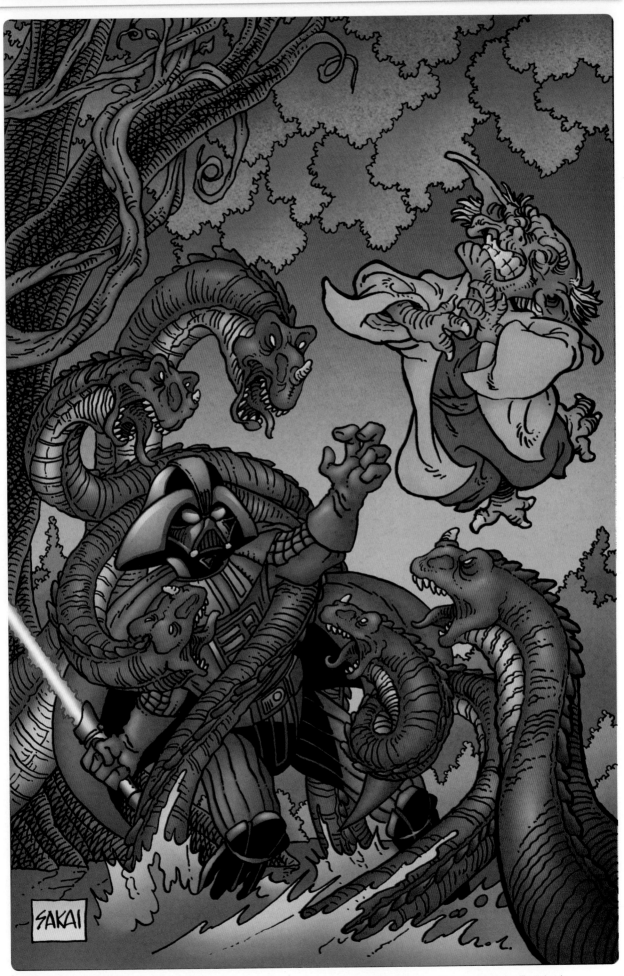

Star Wars #1 Sakai Corner Store Comics Variant—pencils and inks by Stan Sakai, colors by Tom Luth

Star Wars #1 Suayan Hastings Black and White Variant—by Mico Suayan

Star Wars #1 Suayan Hastings Variant—pencils and inks by Mico Suayan, colors by Chris Sotomayor

Princess Leia #1, *Star Wars #1*, and *Darth Vader #1*
Suayan Hastings Variants—pencils and inks by
Mico Suayan, colors by Chris Sotomayor

Princess Leia #1, *Star Wars #1*, and *Darth Vader #1*
Suayan Hastings Black and White Variants—by Mico Suayan

AREN'T YOU A LITTLE SHORT FOR A STORMTROOPER?

Then again, every character on Skottie Young's series of interlocking covers for *Star Wars #1, Darth Vader #1*, and *Princess Leia #1* is a bit on the small side. But that's just the way he likes them—and the same goes for the legion of fans that snap up an ever-growing collection of "Little Marvels" variant covers. The artist and writer has a long career at Marvel, stretching from 2003's *Human Torch* to 2014's *Rocket Raccoon*, with his work in between including a critically acclaimed series of adaptations of Frank L. Baum's Oz stories. But one of his most successful assignments of all would prove to be, of all things, his variant cover for 2012's *Red She-Hulk #58*—the first one to go on sale in a series of covers to celebrate the Marvel NOW! initiative. The eye-catching image, featuring tiny versions of the title character and her co-star, Machine Man, was quickly followed by a similarly kiddified cover for *Uncanny Avengers #1*, and the comic-book industry had its latest red-hot collector trend—still going strong after more than 100 covers.

It's "insane," according to Young. "I thought it would just be ten for the launch of Marvel NOW! Three years later, people are still enjoying them as much I do making them. I just like the fact that people are open to a different, lighthearted take on their favorite characters."

Now the variant craze that took the Marvel Universe by storm has reached a certain other far-off galaxy—and for Young, it's a dream come true. "Like most people my age, I spent a good part of my childhood playing with *Star Wars* toys for hours on end," he says. "I cried like a baby when I realized I left my wampa figure on the radiator, and his leg melted half off. Flash-forward years later, and I get to be a little—pun absolutely intended—part of the *Star Wars* universe by creating my take on these covers. It's surreal." Young has shared his childhood trauma previously, and fans have brought him wampa figures at conventions—just one more reminder of the crazy life of a comic-book artist. But in the future, any such generous fan is bound to be carrying a Young *Star Wars* variant under the other arm.

Star Wars #1 Young Variant—by Skottie Young

Princess Leia #1, *Star Wars #1*, and *Darth Vader #1* Young Variants

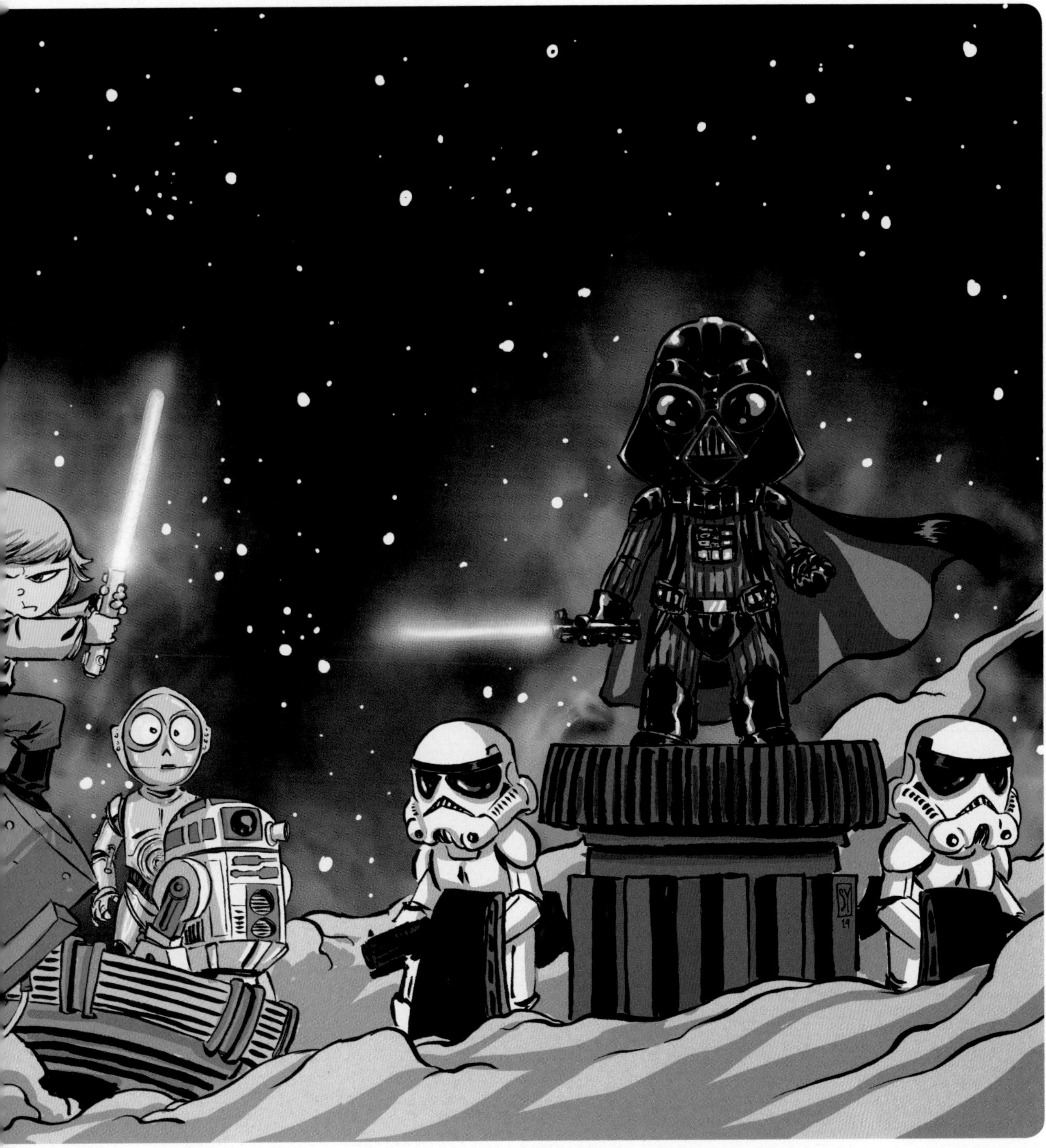

by Skottie Young

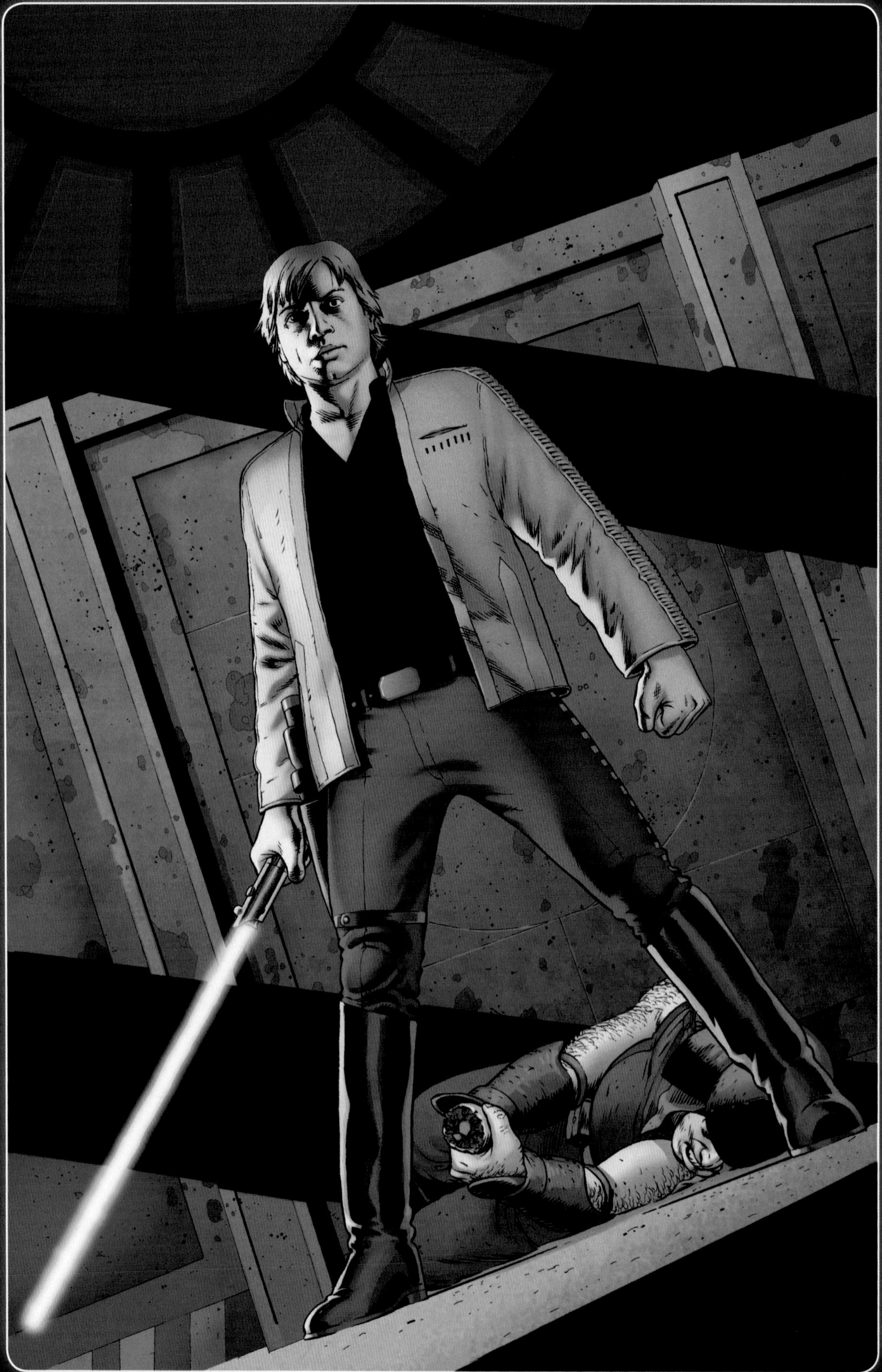

To celebrate the success of the first three titles in Marvel's bold new era of *Star Wars* comic books, Editor Jordan D. White assembled his brain trust—writers Jason Aaron (*Star Wars*), Kieron Gillen (*Darth Vader*), and Mark Waid (*Princess Leia*)—for a roundtable discussion on life, art, Wookieepedia, and the sheer thrill of crafting new tales for that fabled galaxy far, far away.

Jordan D. White: Everyone has a *Star Wars* story, right?

I wasn't alive just yet when the first film hit theaters, and was only five months old when the Empire struck back...but I know my three-year-old self saw *Star Wars* Episode VI *Return of the Jedi* on the big screen—one of the first movies I ever went to. Point being, the original trilogy has been a part of my mental landscape since I first started mapping it out.

And I wanted every toy I could get my hands on—the action figures, the little mini-playsets...and of course, a lightsaber. This was the older lightsaber toy—it didn't extend and retract, but it had a metal spring inside the tube to make noise when you swung it around. It also came with a little certificate you could fill out to become a Jedi Knight. Imagine my mother's surprise when I refused to fill out the form.

"But why not?" she asked. "You love *Star Wars*!"

"Because, Mom," I replied, "if I fill out that form, I'm going to have to fight Darth Vader."

I was no fool.

Little did I know, 30 or so years later, I would be battling with Vader in a slightly different way. Thankfully, he's very receptive to editorial notes.

Kieron Gillen: Much more than his writer...

White: In all seriousness—it's truly been an honor to help bring the *Star Wars* books to life back at Marvel Comics. It's such an inviting and exciting universe to jump into, which is why it continues to capture the imaginations of fans the world over. As you can see in this collection, the comic industry's top artists came out to the siren's song of the Skywalkers' saga.

After all, everyone has a *Star Wars* story, right? So what are yours, guys?

Mark Waid: In 1977, I was a junior in high school and, like most of us, had my regular gang I hung out with on Saturday nights. On one of those fateful autumn evenings, we got together and then—only after we were all crammed into Karen Ticovny's battered Oldsmobile 98, practically on top of one another and on our way to the multiplex—argued about which new movie to see. There was dissension in the ranks, and—by sheer force of personality—I made the deciding edict. I knew that most of us wanted to try that one new film, but I insisted on the other one despite the fact that we knew so much less about it. I promised my friends they'd all be sorry if we missed the one I was dead set on seeing. I swore to them that their choice was lame, but my choice was an event. That they would remember the night we joined together for this movie for the rest of their lives. And I won. Like Moses leading his people to the Promised Land, I marched my friends with utter confidence right into Theater Three. I smiled smugly and shivered with nervous anticipation as the lights went down, pre-basking in the imminent praise of my peers. And sure enough, my reward two hours later was the look of gaping astonishment on everyone's faces as the lights went up, and they realized just what they'd seen—what I'd pushed them toward despite their protestations—the film of our generation: *You Light Up My Life*, starring Didi Conn and Michael Zaslow.

By the time I came out of the bathroom, they'd left me at the theater. I had to call my stepmother for a ride home. Even she wasn't speaking to me. Look, I don't know what to tell you other than no one ever, ever let me pick a movie again—and they were justified. Next Saturday, we saw *Star Wars*...and the Saturday after that...and every Saturday for the rest of the year. In time, my sins were forgiven.

White: At least you were right about them remembering that night.

Gillen: I actually finish up the set here—I was too young to see *Star Wars* in the cinema, but *Empire* was the first movie I ever saw on the big screen. This probably set the tone for all the minor-key, depressing stories of pyrrhic heroism that I seem to have spent my career writing, y'know? In many ways, I have spent my life dumping Han Solo in carbonite.

The strangest thing about seeing it in the cinema was, before the show, they projected TIE fighters on the wall, in very basic light vision. It wouldn't have been lasers, as it was too early for that, but something that looked like that to my five-year-old mind—these iconic shapes just dancing around, outside the screen and infecting the universe.

I have no idea if it actually happened. I mentioned it to my parents, who have no memory. No one I've ever talked to saw anything similar. Part of me wonders whether it was some manner of Grant Morrison-esque fiction/reality-warping experience that has set the route for the rest of my life. A larger part of me wonders whether I've somehow mixed up the classic vector-based *Star Wars* game with my memories of watching the movie.

Jason Aaron: Like Kieron, I don't remember when I first saw the original *Star Wars*. But I vividly remember seeing *Empire* in the theater during its original run. My mom took me and one of my friends and my friend's older brother to our little small-town Alabama one-screen theater. The older brother had seen it before and kept excitedly blurting out spoilers whenever something good was about to happen. "Oh, this part is great. This is when he cuts open the tauntaun. Just watch. You're gonna love it." Thankfully, my mom convinced him to give it a rest, or else my friend's brother may have never made it off of Hoth alive. It wasn't that the kid was trying to be a jerk. He just couldn't contain his excitement for what he was seeing and experiencing. And in the days and years that followed, neither could I.

I honestly don't know if I'd be writing for a living if it wasn't for *Star Wars*. It sparked something in my brain at such a formative age. It was like a shot of space-steroids injected directly into the muscles of my imagination. The first stories I ever created were *Star Wars* stories. But you can't read them, because they weren't written down. They were the stories I was making up in the backyard as I arranged my action figures in various formations and played out the scenarios for dozens of *Star Wars* sequels.

I still have all those same action figures. Only now when I play with them, it's officially work-related research.

Waid: 2015 marks my 30th anniversary in comics, and in that time I've been lucky to be able to contribute to the mythos of not only most of Marvel's heroes, but to dozens of other American touchstones, as well— from Archie Andrews to Superman to Stephen Colbert (it's true). And I will be honest with you, after such a long time, it's easy to relax into it and take those opportunities for granted.

And then I wrote the words "*Princess Leia #1*, Page One, Panel One" and in an instant became overwhelmed with the kind of flop sweat I hadn't known since early in my career. Only then did the enormity of the opportunity sink in. Only then did I realize that I was being entrusted with one of the single most important and most recognizable cultural icons created in the last hundred years. Man, talk about having to up your game. All over the world, readers would be looking at this series to entertain them and to be faithful to the canon, and if there were a single *Star Wars* fan I disappointed—or worse, a young female reader who didn't come away from this wanting to be Princess Leia—I would fail.

Luckily, I could not have asked for better creative partners. The Dodsons gave life and bounce and energy to my scripts, and elevated them beyond measure, and colorist Jordie Bellaire transformed our work into one of the best-looking comics I've ever been a part of.

Gillen: I'm actually surprised my brain didn't just break. As I said, *Empire* was the first movie I saw in the cinema. That means it's resting right at the root of the big pulpish part of my brain. The idea that I'm actually writing a story that is the lead-in to that movie is... well, I can't process it even now. It just doesn't seem something feasible. If I went back in time and grabbed that five-year-old me on the way out and told him it... well, my parents would have called the police as a strange bearded man has just grabbed their five-year-old son. But in a less literal sense, he simply wouldn't have believed it. It's fantastical.

As such, I don't think I've processed it even now, and that's actually an advantage. I haven't been overwhelmed by the responsibility at all, as I don't really believe it's happening. I just do it. How instinctive it's been is the big surprise. A lot of Vader comes right from my gut.

Aaron: When I sat down to write page one of *Star Wars #1*, I literally put on the John Williams score. I figured it's not every day you get to write a *Star Wars #1*, so I wanted to do it up right. I listened to that score, and the first words I wrote were: "A long time ago in a galaxy far, far away...." And after that, it was off to the races. And I haven't stopped smiling since.

Gillen: I actually have a playlist for *Darth Vader* that just consists of the "Imperial March" on repeat.

White: Kieron, Jason, and I were lucky enough to get a tour of the Lucasfilm Archives at the Skywalker Ranch, where they have tons of the original props and costumes for the entire saga (not to mention *Indiana Jones, Willow*, and even *Howard the Duck*). That was a *super* incredible experience, seeing up close these objects that had only existed on screen. At the end, they asked if there was anything we had not seen that we'd wanted to see...and I suddenly realized we hadn't seen a mouse droid! Sure enough, they brought me over to where they had one, and let me tell you...misleading name. Those puppies are bigger than I expected.

Aaron: It felt like we were all kids again, walking through those archives, oohing and aahing at everything we saw. I'm not sure any of us needed reminding about what this job was really all about, but if we did, that trip did the trick. I know John Cassaday and I in particular walked away more determined than ever that our book should give readers the same feelings we'd had when we were kids, first experiencing the world of *Star Wars*. We wanted our book to look and feel and sound just like those original movies. We wanted it to seem like it was 1977, and you'd just walked out of seeing *Star Wars*, and somebody had handed you this comic and said, "Here, this is the next chapter of that story." I think walking through those archives really crystallized everything in my brain. It was also just flat-out cool. It was really hard not to grab a lightsaber and chase Kieron around the room, whacking at him.

Gillen: The speeder bike is what threw me. I had a look at the back to see if it had the button that made it explode, like the toys—but no.

White: I've widely trumpeted—much to the shock of those who think I should be ashamed of it—that my favorite character in *Star Wars* is C-3PO. In truth, I am partial to droids in general, but Threepio I find so delightful. Yeah, he is a coward. And yeah, he messes things up a lot. But he does it in the best ways. Of course, now I am also super-fond of his doppelganger in the *Darth Vader* series, Triple-Zero. All the charm of a protocol droid with 1,000 times the murder. Who are some of your favorite characters, either from the screen or to write?

Waid: My favorite character to write was Nien Nunb. I'm not joking. My second favorite was Evaan, the X-wing pilot who accompanies Leia on her missions. She was another lesson in how dedicated the *Star Wars* fans are: Though she'd never appeared before *Princess Leia #1*, within 24 hours of that issue going on sale, Evaan already had a Wookieepedia entry that, somehow, had a higher word count than did my script.

Gillen: Oh man! Seeing stuff go on Wookieepedia has been fascinating. I was looking at Boba Fett's page, thinking about him, and hit a little bit of the timeline that confused me, as I didn't recognize it. It took me a few seconds to realize it was actually the canon I'd added at the end of *Darth Vader #1*.

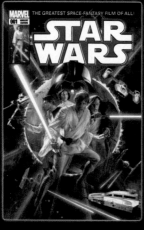

Gillen: Favorite characters? Tricky. Vader is an obvious thing to say, but doesn't mean it's not true. The hardest character to write has been Boba. Jason and I were talking about how in our few appearances, we've already had him say more than he ever said in the movies. Every time I have him speak, it feels somewhat sacrilegious.

The character I'm most like is basically Jabba the Hutt. My mostly platonic life partner, Jamie McKelvie, often describes our relationship as Jabba the Hutt and Salacious Crumb, with him whispering in my ear.

Aaron: Thanks so much for that visual, Kieron.

Is it any surprise that I love writing Han? I think every kid my age wanted to grow up to be Han Solo—because whether he shot first or not, he'll always be the coolest.

But really, it's hard to choose a favorite. I'm lucky in that I'm basically writing a team book, so I never have to choose. I try my best to give big moments to everybody. So I've had a blast writing Chewie kicking butt, Jabba pontificating, old Ben Kenobi wrestling with

his emotions, and C-3PO insulting everybody around him. Much like Mark Waid, Threepio always dishes out the best insults.

White: Well, Mark Waid is widely known as the mindless philosopher of the comics industry. But no—we don't need insults here, we need compliments! Of all the covers we did for these *Star Wars* books so far, what are your favorites?

Waid: My favorite of all the *Princess Leia* covers—and trust me, this was a hard choice to make—is the Skottie Young variant on #1. It's spirited, it's fun to gaze at, it captures the character—and despite Skottie's style, it's a great likeness!

Of the new *Star Wars* covers overall, my favorite is Alex Ross's recreation of the original Marvel *Star Wars #1* cover. The remarkable fact of the matter is that this particular cover, if you're holding the comic in your hands, is a reproduction of a painting of a drawing of an image of a line drawing from 1977, and it is due to Alex's miraculous talent that it nonetheless remains so

lifelike that his brushstrokes make you feel as if you're standing on the set of the movie.

White: Yeah, Alex's cover of *Star Wars #1* is terrific… but I think I prefer his *Darth Vader #1* cover. It's a completely unexpected shot that nonetheless feels perfect. I love it.

Oooh, I also really loved Daniel Acuña's cover for *Star Wars #1*, the homage to the first appearance of the Punisher with Boba Fett and Han. Super fun.

On *Princess Leia #1*, I think my fave is Greg Horn's propaganda cover: "A Million Voices Cried Out—Don't Be Silent Now!"

Gillen: *Darth Vader* had an incredible selection—if I had to pick one, I'd go for Mike Del Mundo's cover. Mike's work is always beautiful, but what gets me is his ideas. I'm a big fan of work with a conceptual element to it, and his *Vader* one was right from that. The sheer oppressive size of the Vader helmet capturing him as an icon before you realize the tiny Anakin is visible,

slightly pensive, between the grill. A literal showing of the helmet as a prison. Mike just kills me.

Aaron: Yeah, Mike Del Mundo is all kinds of amazing. My favorite cover in this book is actually Mike's variant for *Star Wars #1*, which has Artoo projecting a hologram of the entire cast. I need that as a poster on my wall.

I also gotta confess a weird soft spot for the cover that features Jaxxon, the big, green star-hopping bunny from the original Marvel *Star Wars* series. The cover shows the poor guy trying to sneak into the *Star Wars #1* release party, but the rest of the cast won't let him. Poor Jaxxon. Maybe the tide will turn for him once Jordan finally approves my pitch for a Jaxxon/Jar Jar buddy-cop book.

And I really love all those various action-figure variants—because for me, they're a nice reminder of what this is all about: a kid playing with toys, while a universe of stories explodes through his brain. Once upon a time, I was that kid. And now I'm one of the guys making up the stories for real. I don't ever wanna lose sight of how cool that is.

Star Wars #2 Cassaday Sketch Variant—by John Cassaday

Star Wars #2—pencils and inks by John Cassaday, colors by Laura Martin

Star Wars #2 Aragonés Variant—pencils and inks by Sergio Aragonés, colors by Chris Sotomayor

Star Wars #2 Chaykin Variant—pencils and inks by Howard Chaykin, colors by Jesus Aburtov

Star Wars #2 Christopher Action Figure Variant—by John Tyler Christopher

Star Wars #2 Ramos Mile High Comics Variant—pencils and inks by Humberto Ramos, colors by Edgar Delgado   109

Star Wars #2 Yu Variant—pencils and inks by Leinil Francis Yu, colors by Jason Keith

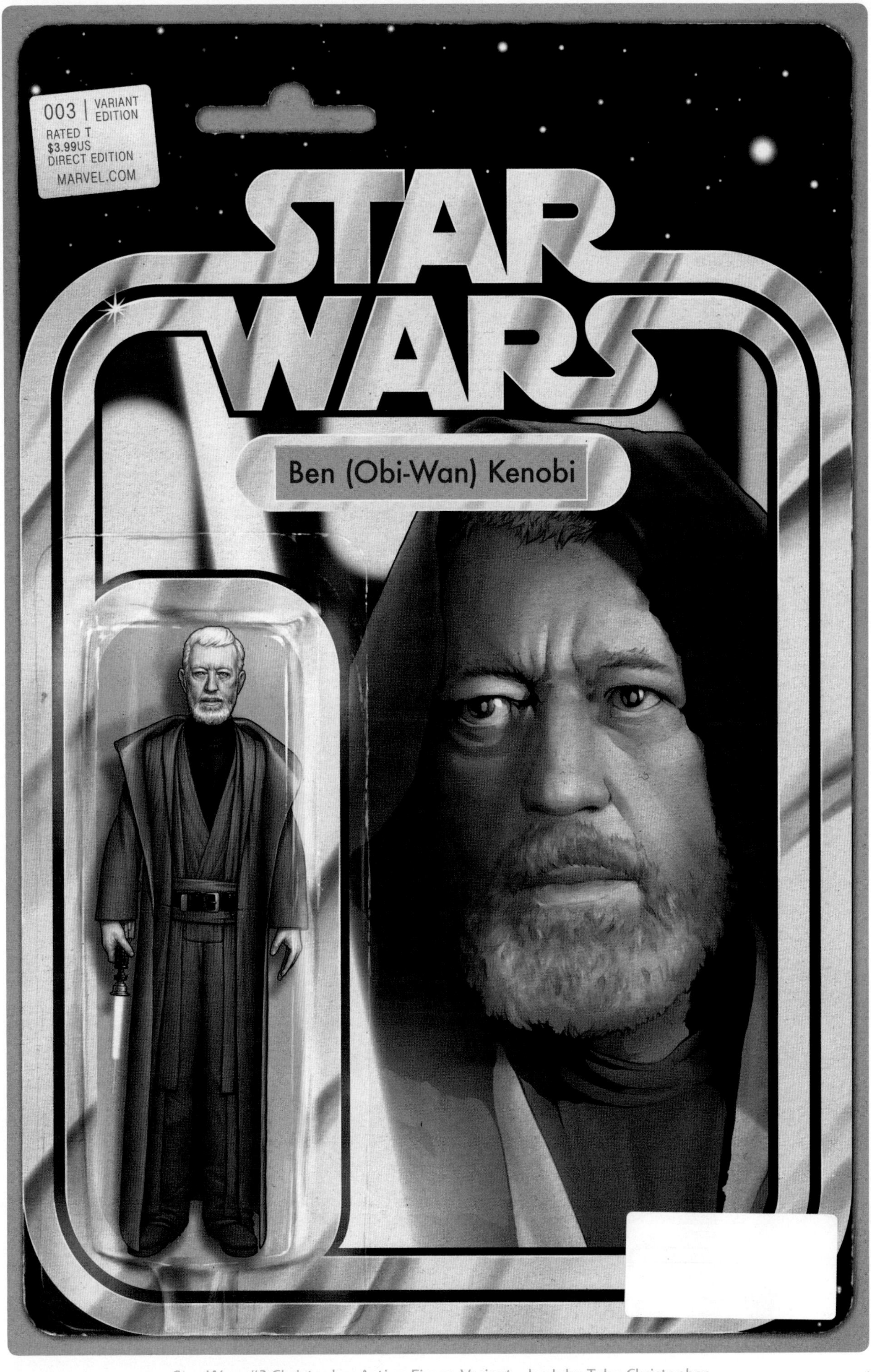
003 | VARIANT EDITION
RATED T
$3.99US
DIRECT EDITION
MARVEL.COM
STAR WARS
Ben (Obi-Wan) Kenobi

Star Wars #3 Christopher Action Figure Variant—by John Tyler Christopher

Star Wars #3 Cassaday Sketch Variant—by John Cassaday

Star Wars #3—pencils and inks by John Cassaday, colors by Laura Martin

Star Wars #3 Ramos Mile High Comics Variant—pencils and inks by Humberto Ramos, colors by Edgar Delgado

Star Wars #3 Yu Variant—pencils and inks by Leinil Francis Yu, colors by Marte Gracia

Star Wars #4 Cassaday Sketch Variant—by John Cassaday

Star Wars #4—pencils and inks by John Cassaday, colors by Laura Martin

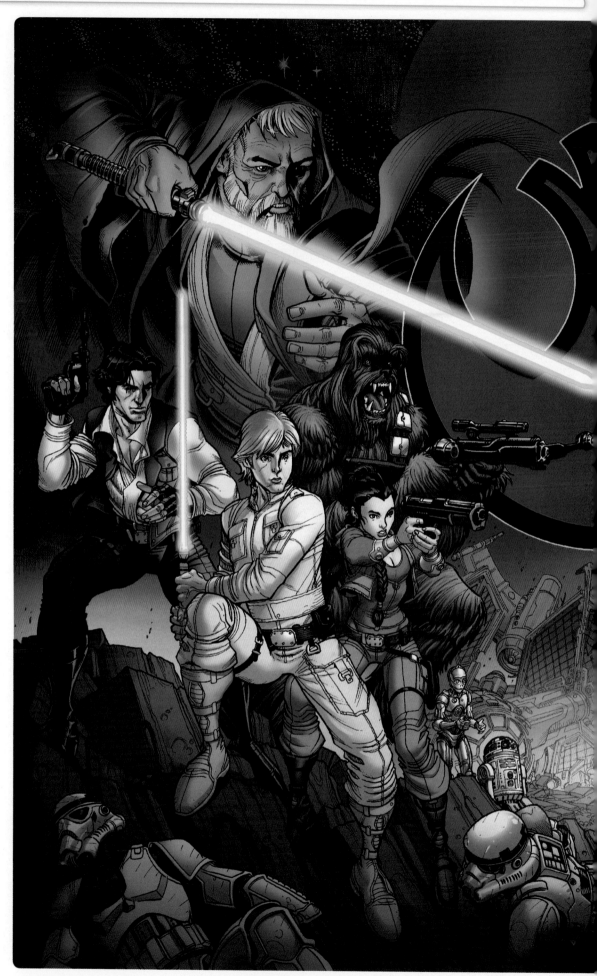

Star Wars #4 Bradshaw GameStop Connecting Variants

pencils and inks by Nick Bradshaw, colors by Guru-eFX

Star Wars #4 Christopher Action Figure Variant—by John Tyler Christopher

STAR WARS

004 | JTC VARIANT EDITION
RATED T
$3.99US
DIRECT EDITION
MARVEL.COM

Boba Fett

Star Wars #4 Christopher Boba Fett Variant—by John Tyler Christopher

Star Wars #4 Camuncoli Variant—pencils and inks by Giuseppe Camuncoli, colors by Israel Gonzalez

Star Wars #4 Noto Bam Variant—by Phil Noto

Star Wars #4 Ramos Mile High Comics Variant—pencils and inks by Humberto Ramos, colors by Edgar Delgado

STAR WARS

See-Threepio (C-3PO)

Star Wars #5 Christopher Action Figure Variant—by John Tyler Christopher

Star Wars #5 Cassaday Sketch Variant—by John Cassaday

Star Wars #5—pencils and inks by John Cassaday, colors by Laura Martin

Star Wars #5 Ramos Mile High Comics Variant—pencils and inks by Humberto Ramos, colors by Edgar Delgado

Star Wars #6—pencils and inks by John Cassaday, colors by Laura Martin

006 | VARIANT EDITION
RATED T
$3.99US
DIRECT EDITION
MARVEL.COM

STAR WARS

TM

Artoo-Detoo (R2-D2)

Star Wars #6 Christopher Action Figure Variant—by John Tyler Christopher

Star Wars #6 Ramos Mile High Comics Variant—pencils and inks by Humberto Ramos, colors by Edgar Delgado

Star Wars #1–6 Ramos Mile High
Comics Variants—pencils and inks by
Humberto Ramos, colors by Edgar Delgado

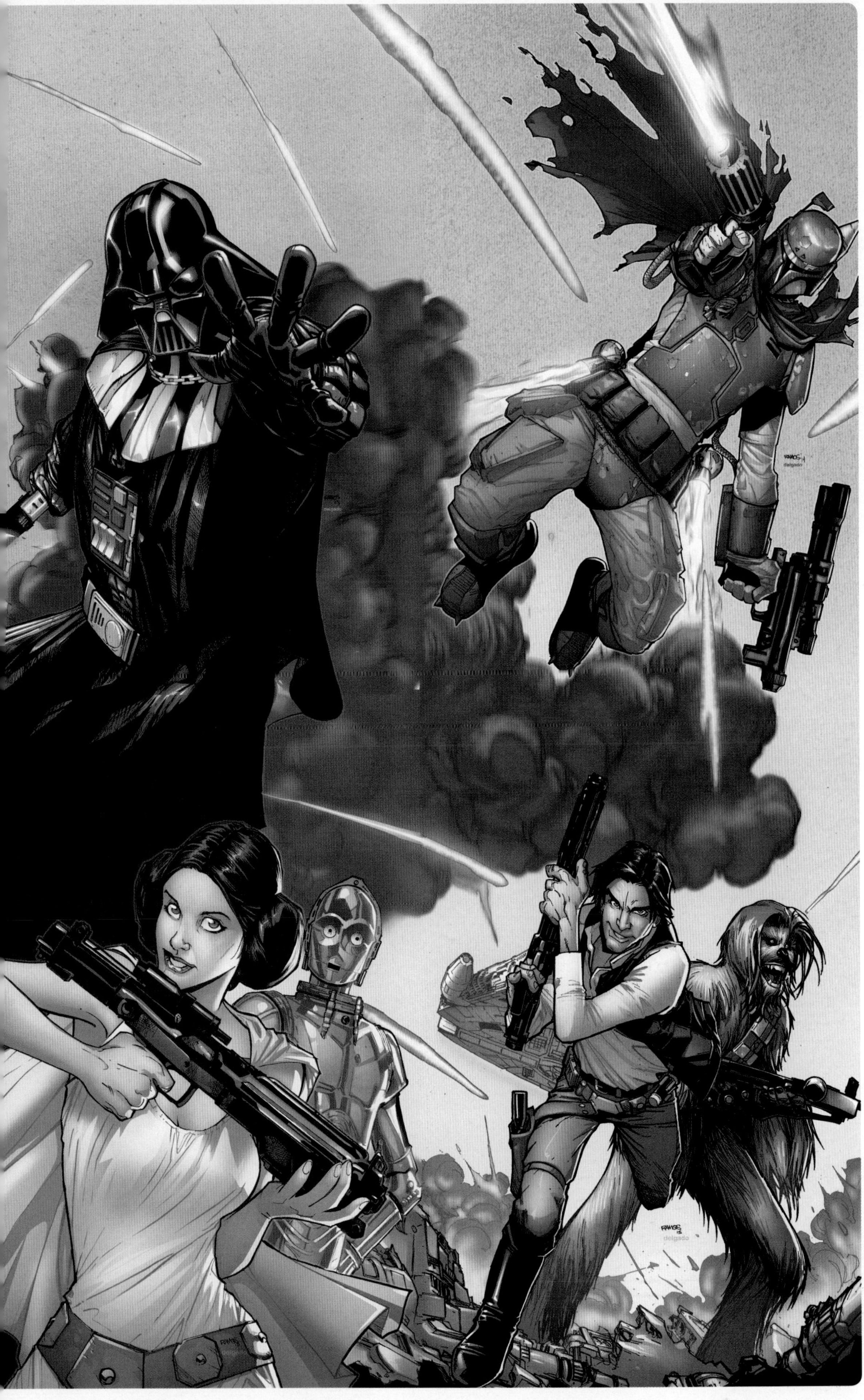

GIVE YOURSELF TO THE DARK SIDE...

...and do it gladly. For all the wide-eyed heroism of Luke, the brave resilience of Leia, the rugged charm of Han, so many of the greatest moments in the *Star Wars* series belong to the galaxy's more ruthless individuals. The scum and villainy, if you will—with all the fear, anger, and suffering that follows in their wake. And no enemy of the Rebellion is greater than the Empire's ebon-clad enforcer, Darth Vader. Not that this Sith Lord, the Emperor's deadly right hand, would cast himself as the evil one. And nor would Kieron Gillen, the writer tasked with taking Vader's story into his first ongoing series. "No one is a villain," Gillen says, addressing

how he gets inside the head of one of cinema's most iconic adversaries. "Everyone does everything for reasons." Gillen's first step in plotting a course for Vader following the events of *A New Hope* was a close viewing of the films with an analytic eye, considering at all points what his title character would be thinking and feeling. One key scene for Gillen was when Vader briefed the bounty hunters in *Star Wars* Episode V *The Empire Strikes Back*. "That said a lot about him," Gillen says, "oddly, including how much of a micromanager he is. More importantly, it said that he knew these people and their world. That gave me what is pretty much the core of my story."

When it comes to putting words in Vader's mouth, of course, it's impossible not to hear one of the most memorable voices in films in one's head. "Don't underestimate the James Earl Jones element," Gillen says. "The great joy of a character with such an iconic performance is that you can tell easily if something is off. You ask yourself, could you imagine James Earl Jones ever saying that?" The secret to Vader, Gillen has found,

is that less is more. "You spend time reverse-analyzing things. What are the key Vader-esque moments? How are they constructed? What sort of feed-lines does he respond to? Why, exactly, does 'I find your lack of faith disturbing' work as well as it does? You can write a lot of dialogue that sounds like Vader, but the problem would be that it's too much dialogue. I delete as much as I can. One reason why I add the supporting cast is that it means they can do a lot of the expositional speech, which means Vader can be even more silent." As in the films, that allows for the Sith Lord's full menace to be demonstrated visually, with series artist Salvador Larroca eminently capable of capturing him in all his cinematic glory. "In terms of sci-fi, he's the number-one character to me, maybe level with the Terminator," Larroca says. "I'm aware that when I draw Vader, the whole world is watching, so I try to be religiously careful when I draw him and move him. Vader is not a man who moves in a useless way. I only try to match what I see in the films." Vader is an "iconic bad guy," according to Larroca—and like so many adversaries in Marvel Comics, he's not a straightforward, one-dimensional villain. "He's a fallen angel, a good guy that became bad because of circumstances," Larroca adds.

Painter Alex Ross, who contributes a trio of variant covers for *Darth Vader #1*, ranks Vader "right next to Dracula as the most well-known villain throughout the

world." But he adds, "Drawing him is a challenge for accuracy, since I want to make sure I get that damned helmet right, which looks different on almost every toy I have of it."

Darth Vader cover artist Adi Granov shares their enthusiasm. "Darth Vader is the greatest villain of modern fiction, in my opinion," Granov says. "I can't think of a single other character who is so iconic and so wonderfully realized. The complexity of Darth Vader, his descent into darkness and his eventual redemption, his motivation, the design, and the machinery that keeps him alive are what make him so fascinating. I don't think *Star Wars* would be anywhere near as appealing if the villains weren't as compelling as they are. In my view, they are more interesting than the heroes, with much more complex and absorbing histories. Technically, the most interesting heroes are the rogues, like Han Solo, as pure heroes often need a great antagonist to make them come alive." One of the other villains who has proved particularly popular with cover artists for the new *Star Wars* titles is the bounty hunter Boba Fett, who has achieved cult status despite only a relatively brief appearance in *The Empire Strikes Back* and a seemingly ignominious end in *Return of the Jedi*. For Gillen, who quickly found a place for Boba Fett in his *Darth Vader* series, it's that lack of screen time that has fueled the character's fame: "His appeal is at least in part due to his scarcity. His is an incredible design, and we see so little of it, which creates a real hunger. The other element is that the camera treats him as an important figure. Just how he's framed, his actions, how he's shot. The film tells us he's a big deal—and he is."

Granov, who depicts the bounty hunter on a particularly striking *Star Wars #1* cover, adds, "I think Boba Fett's popularity primarily comes from the fact that he is

so mysterious, obviously helped by the fact that he has a great helmet and a jetpack. Everything about him seems to be thought out and designed to a level that isn't reflected in his screen time. Just look at his spaceship—it's an amazing design, but you see very little of it. He's presented as a really important villain and has an important role, but the fact the movies don't deliver on the possibilities has really sparked the imagination of fans."

Ross, who features the Mandalorian warrior on one of his *Darth Vader #1* covers, had a different reason for doing so. "My choice of doing a solo Boba Fett variant was simply to acknowledge my favorite buried part of *Star Wars* history: the 1978 *Star Wars Holiday Special*," he explains. "This televised Christmas special that assembled all of the movie's cast is especially noteworthy for its introduction of Boba Fett in his first appearance ever. It featured him in cartoon form only, but it made a huge impression on fans like me, and it clearly hinted at how important he should become in the movie sequels to follow. My illustration is a clear signal to those who have seen it. I placed him atop the weirdly shaped dinosaur-like creature he was first seen riding in on, and I also show the green sky and neighboring planets (or moons) that were in the scene. The heavy shadow I laid upon Boba was meant to disguise the colors that differentiate between his animated design and the later live-action version."

With more of the iconic nemeses fans love to hate, such as the Emperor and Jabba the Hutt, also appearing in *Darth Vader*, it's a good time to be a bad guy—and some new faces are getting in on the act. They include the Wookiee bounty hunter Black Krrsantan, the homicidal droids Triple-Zero and BT-1, and the rogue archaeologist Doctor Aphra—each in their own way a dark reflection of a rebel hero. "I thought that was both fun and a useful literary construct," Gillen explains. "We're the mirror book to Jason Aaron and John Cassaday's *Star Wars*. Vader fundamentally takes the Luke role—and like Luke, he needs a cast around him. Clearly it can't be the same cast, as Vader is far from a callow farm boy, but that dynamic is deeply *Star Wars*. My aim was to do an *Empire*-set book that feels like *Star Wars*—with all its wit, high adventure and capital-R Romance. If you just do a straight *Empire* book, it'd end up feeling fascist, gun-metal gray. I have to attack it from a different angle." Gillen plans to keep bringing on the bad guys, building a group of "rivals" to pit against the rebels, but is conscious each new character he introduces must fit into a richly defined galaxy. "Trying to find a way to make a character feel like it's part of the *Star Wars* universe is a big thing," he says. "With one character, Cylo, we push that quite close to the edge, but hopefully stop at the right spot. The visuals are a huge part of that. With a character like Tulon Voidgazer—my favorite of the rivals, I suspect—you can see that we're taking established parts of the *Star Wars* visuals and remixing them in a way that becomes their own thing entirely. Something new, but something recognizable." That's a philosophy that applies across the Marvel titles, and one exemplified by their covers, including the following from the first six issues of *Darth Vader*. Savor them, and realize the power of the dark side.

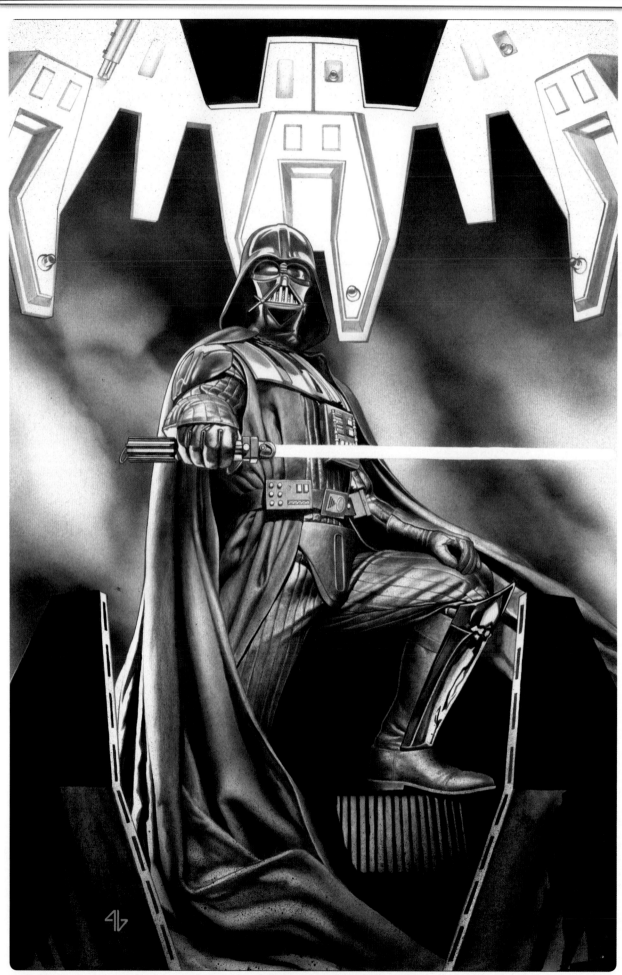

Darth Vader #1 Granov ComicsPRO Black and White Variant—by Adi Granov

Darth Vader #1—by Adi Granov

Darth Vader #1 Movie Variant

Darth Vader #1 Bianchi GameStop Variant—by Simone Bianchi

Darth Vader #1 Brooks Midtown Comics Black and White Variant—by Mark Brooks

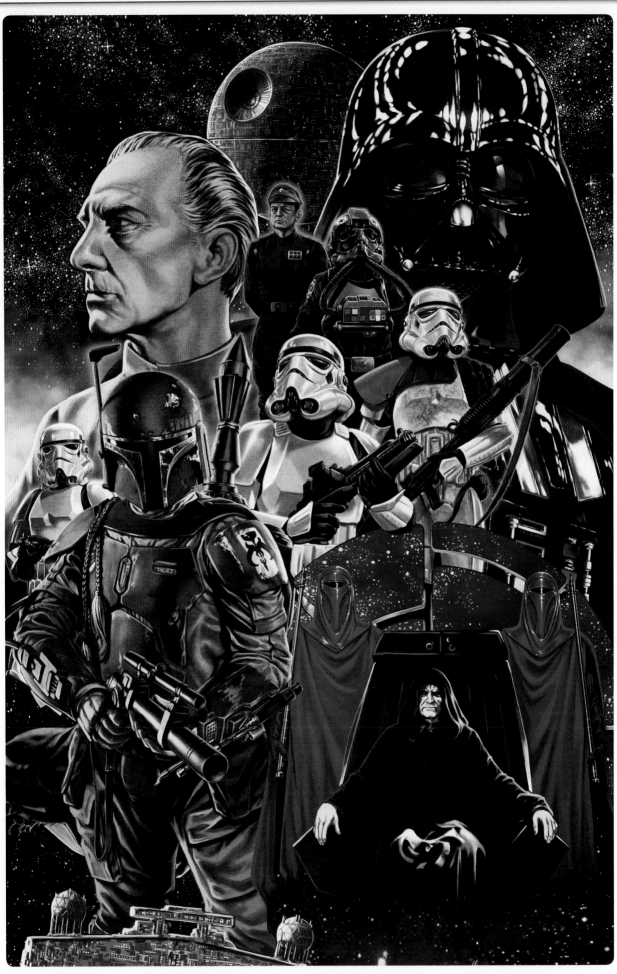

Darth Vader #1 Brooks Midtown Comics Variant—by Mark Brooks

Darth Vader #1 Campbell Connecting Variant—pencils and inks by J. Scott Campbell, colors by Nei Ruffino

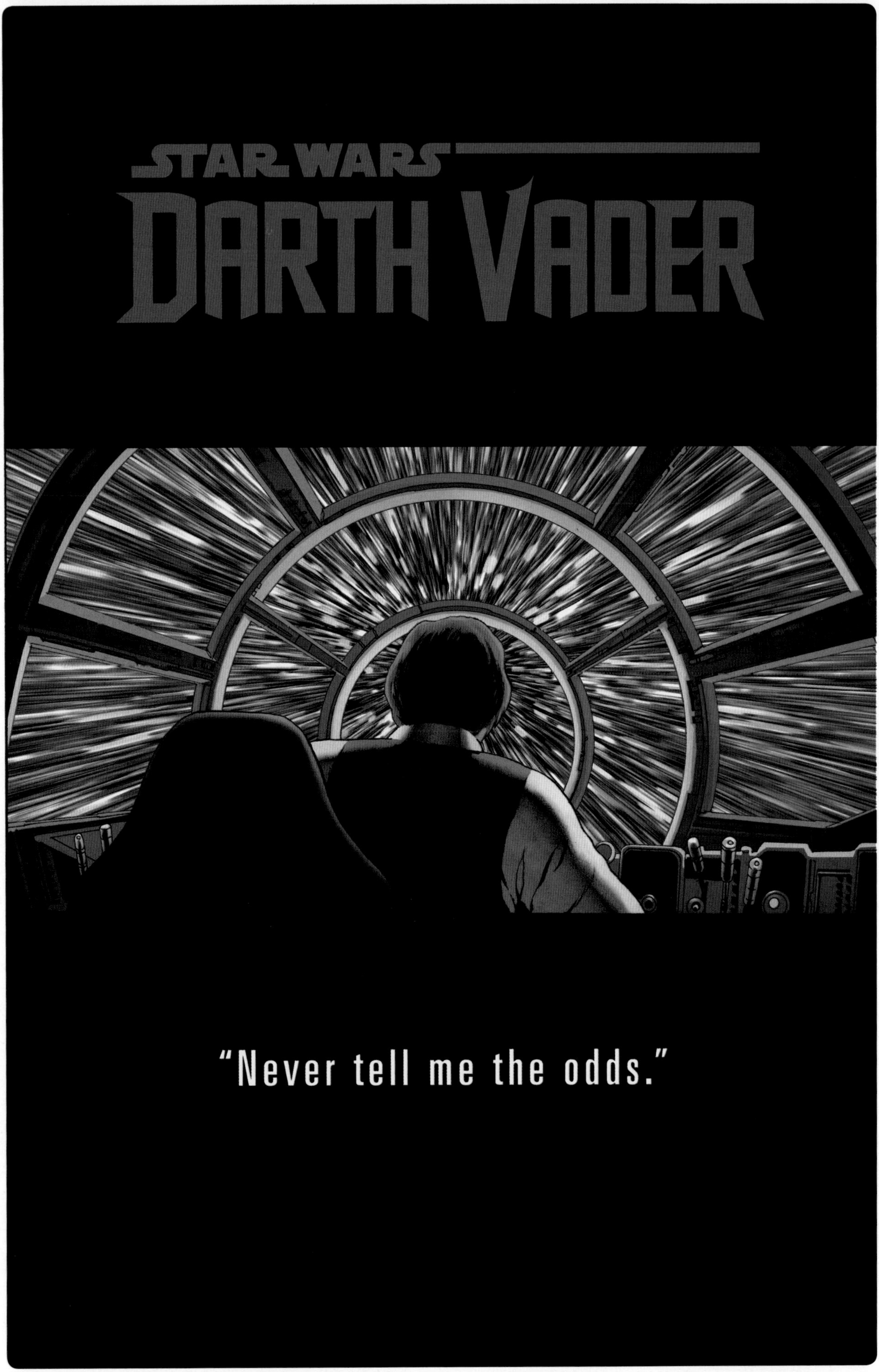
STAR WARS
DARTH VADER
"Never tell me the odds."

Darth Vader #1 Cassaday Teaser Variant—pencils and inks by John Cassaday, colors by Laura Martin

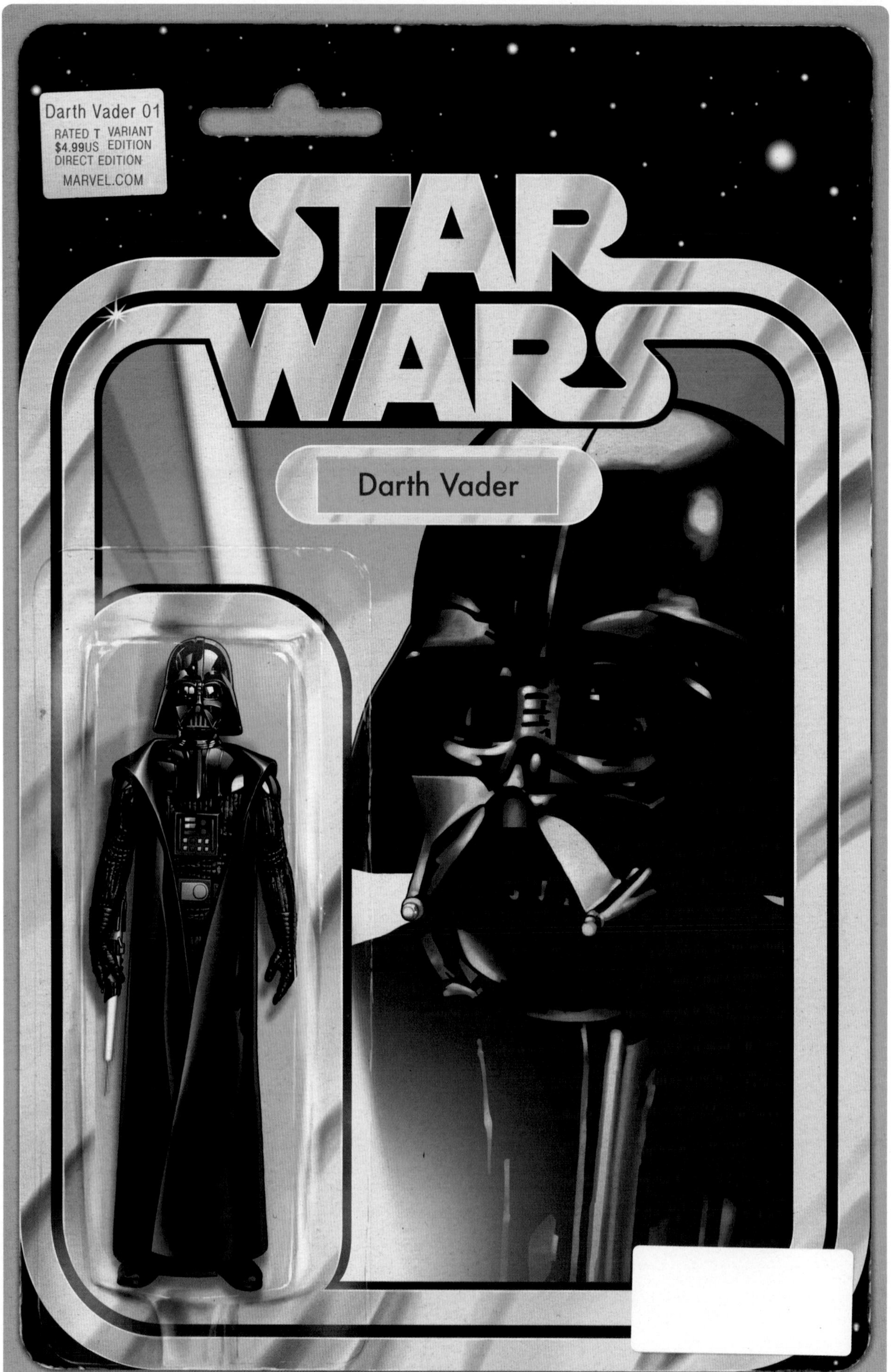
Darth Vader 01
RATED T VARIANT
$4.99US EDITION
DIRECT EDITION
MARVEL.COM
STAR WARS
Darth Vader

 Darth Vader #1 Christopher Action Figure Variant—by John Tyler Christopher

Darth Vader #1 Del Mundo Variant—by Mike Del Mundo

Darth Vader #1 Horn GameStop Variant—by Greg Horn

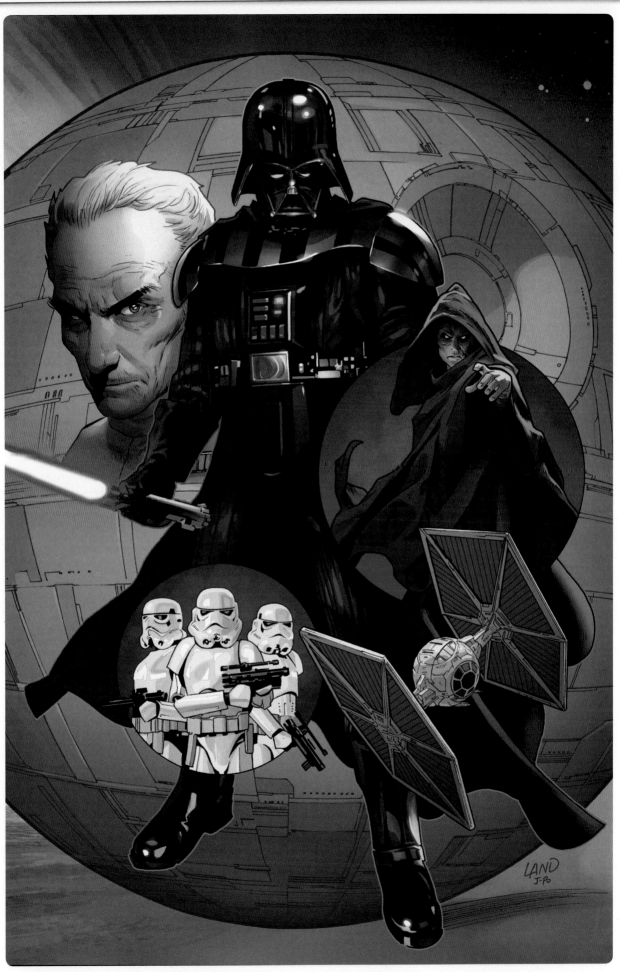

Darth Vader #1 Land Dynamite Entertainment Variant—pencils and inks by Greg Land, colors by Justin Ponsor

Darth Vader #1 Larroca Newbury Comics Variant—pencils and inks by Salvador Larroca, colors by Edgar Delgado

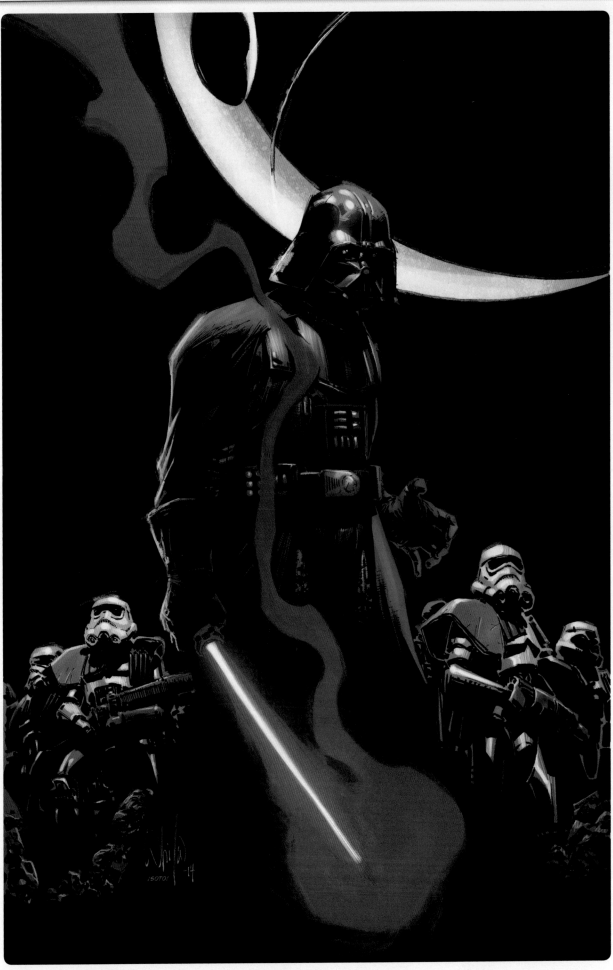

Darth Vader #1 Portacio Classic Variant—pencils and inks by Whilce Portacio, colors by Chris Sotomayor

THERE IS NO TRY...

...not for Alex Ross. He is an artist who does. Having redrawn the boundaries of comic-book illustration during the 1990s on *Marvels* and *Kingdom Come*, for Marvel and DC, respectively, Ross has cemented his reputation as one of the field's most celebrated creators. His covers have graced the titles of virtually every icon of super-hero storytelling. In recent years, his paintings have proven the ideal adornment to celebrate Marvel's landmark anniversaries and groundbreaking first issues. His unique style somehow blends the classic flavor of Golden, Silver, and Bronze Age art with thrillingly modern realism, resulting in gallery-worthy work that appeals to old and new fans alike. All of which made him a perfect fit for Marvel's new *Star Wars* launches, with a trio of Ross covers for each of the inaugural issues of *Star Wars*, *Darth Vader*, and *Princess Leia*.

"I was seven years old when *Star Wars* came out in 1977," Ross recalls. "I remember getting the tabloid-size adaptation, drawn by Howard Chaykin, before I saw the movie in the theater. A big part of my memory of seeing it was that, for however exciting it was to me, my dad fell asleep midway through the film." Though Ross's focus, in terms of both collecting and art, shifted toward super heroes, he believes the characters of *Star Wars* share equal status with the titans of comics history. "*Star Wars* is cinematic proof of the appeal that comic books, science fiction, and fantasy have to everyone," he says. "The films were ahead of their time, to the era we're now in, where this kind of over-the-top escapist entertainment reigns supreme. *Star Wars* was a callback to the stories that were popular in comic strips and movie serials in the early 20th century. George Lucas simply reminded people of the power that material had, and how effective and timeless it was."

Ross has depicted the cast of *Star Wars* several times in his career, and always finds it a challenge. "Drawing and painting the actors and characters from the *Star Wars* pantheon is more intimidating than just about anything else," he says. "Not only can everyone tell whether you captured them right, but most fans can recognize your photo reference if you use any pre-existing shots. For one thing, you have a ridiculous number of pieces by Drew Struzan that you can't hope to compete with. For another, the faces of Mark Hamill, Carrie Fisher, and particularly Harrison Ford are three of the hardest likenesses to capture exactly. Their faces are so unique as to be downright weird—no offense, everybody."

To achieve something different, Ross often seeks to base his work on angles of the actors' heads he has not seen as often, with lighting unlike his reference material. "This is where the many modern dolls and statues of the actors come in handy," he adds. "I pose them however I like and try to match up their believability with what the frames of film look like in contrast."

Here, Ross explains how he applied this approach to one of his *Darth Vader #1* variant covers.

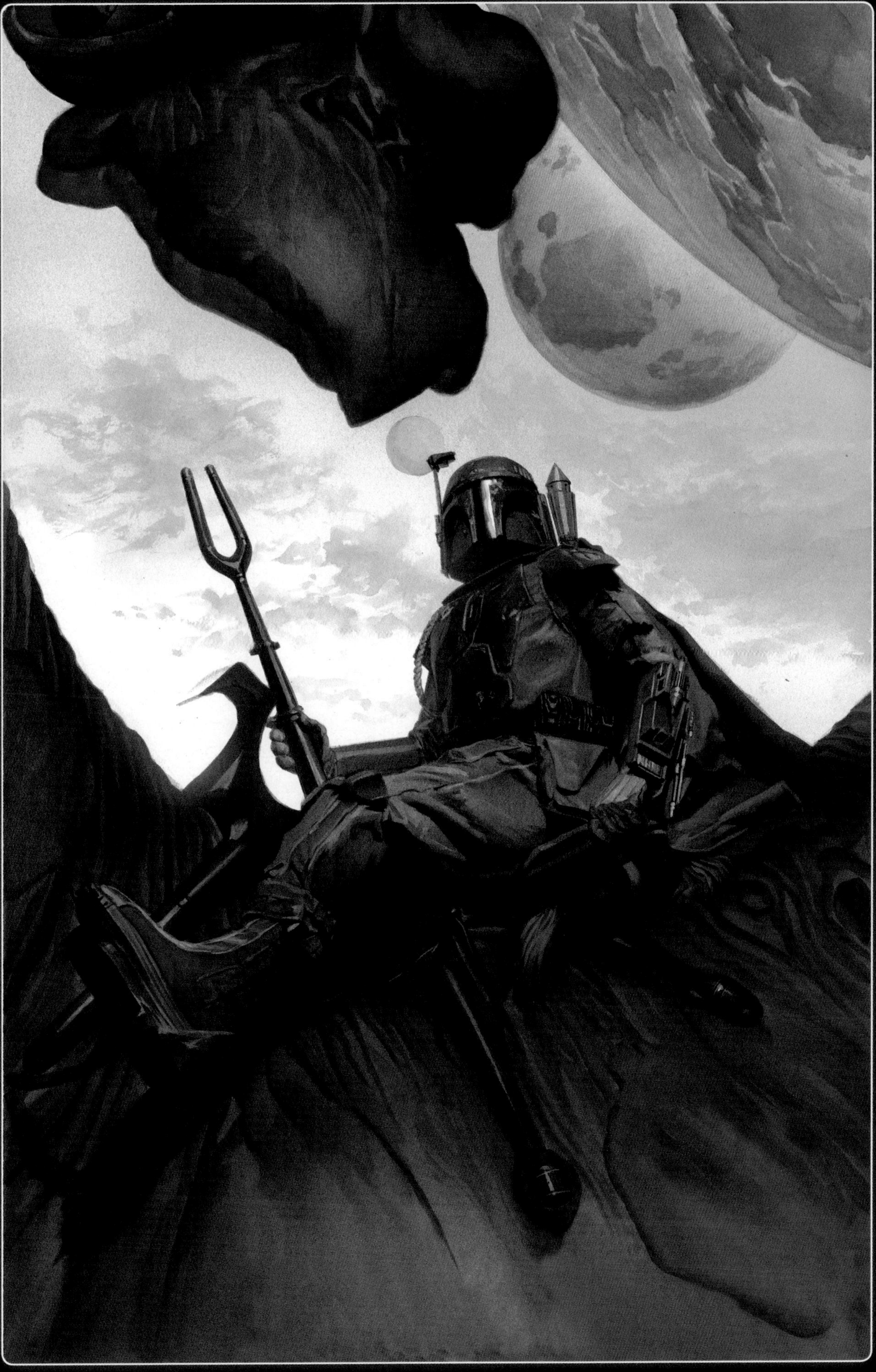

Darth Vader #1 AlexRossStore.com Variant—by Alex Ross

"In doing any of the covers I've done for *Star Wars*, I would first think back to any images that inspire me. Since I've done a few paintings of Darth Vader before, I needed to dig further than my first impulse, which I may have already painted, and recall something that another artist did that struck me in my youth. In this case, a black-and-white piece made by my favorite *Star Wars* artist, Tom Jung, came to mind from the back cover of the first movie's soundtrack album. This ghostly, spattered image always impressed me, and I figured that I could emulate the style of it without replicating the composition."

SKETCHING

"Darth Vader's pose is a challenge in finding something that hopefully hasn't been done before, or to death. I was thinking of thrusting downward with the lightsaber to be different from all of the sword-tip-upheld shots I and others have done. The crouching, samurai-like pose is vaguely referential to that aspect of his design. Also, to be honest, I was thinking a bit about Adi Granov's famous Iron Man-punching-the-ground pose. If I had known when I was doing this that he was producing a similar piece with Boba Fett for his *Star Wars #1* variant, I would have gone another way. The final thumbnail drawing is four by six inches and is what was blown up for the sketch variant cover."

REFERENCE

"Doing art based on *Star Wars* characters became exponentially easier with the great number of realistic toys and statues made in the last decade or so. Now artists like me can position a figure, light it, and photograph it with a very movie-accurate result. When so much art over the last 30 years was made from publicity photos and screen-capture shots, you would see a lot of the same likenesses repeated. Now we can pose this newer, well-sculpted reference material to achieve a different look, hopefully.

"The posing of the background stormtroopers was pretty straightforward, as the dolls I have look pretty perfect, even though I'm not sure how accurate I had their hand positions on those weapons. I checked at least that these guys did have some left-hand holding as well as right in the original films.

"In almost all photos I take for my work, I want to see how the real human body can match the drawings I've mocked up. Kneeling down in the crouched position I placed Vader in taught me some practical limitations. Posing a highly accurate doll would provide most of the costume detail even though I couldn't fully bend it into the contorted position. Darth also has a broad armor codpiece that I was knowingly compromising the integrity of. It would not likely allow him to bend all the way into this dramatic pose. In researching what limits there are, a realist like me has to choose how much I want to compromise my vision for said reality constraints."

Star Wars (2013) #1 and #3–#4— by Alex Ross, originally published by Dark Horse Comics

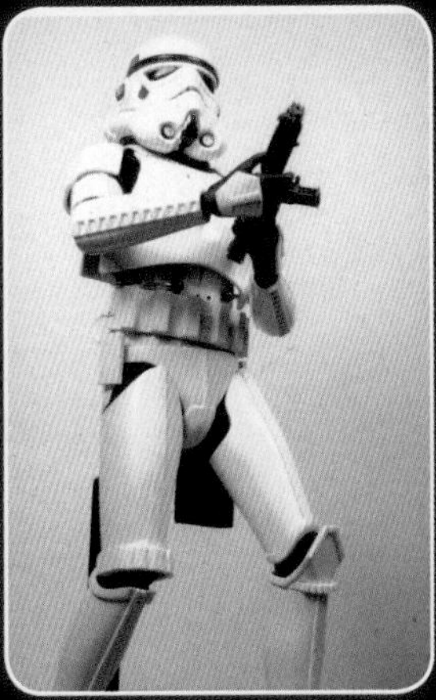

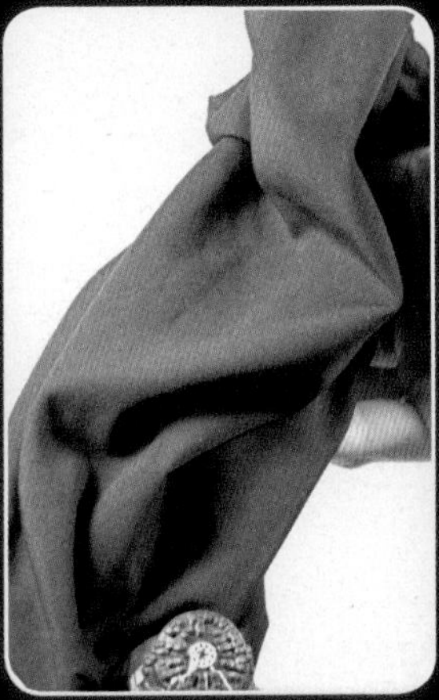

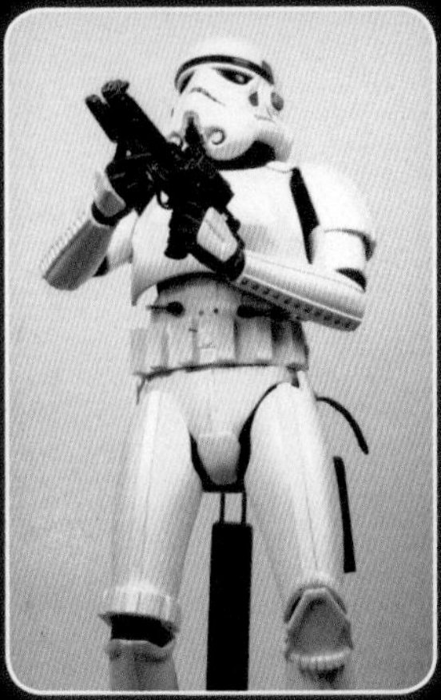

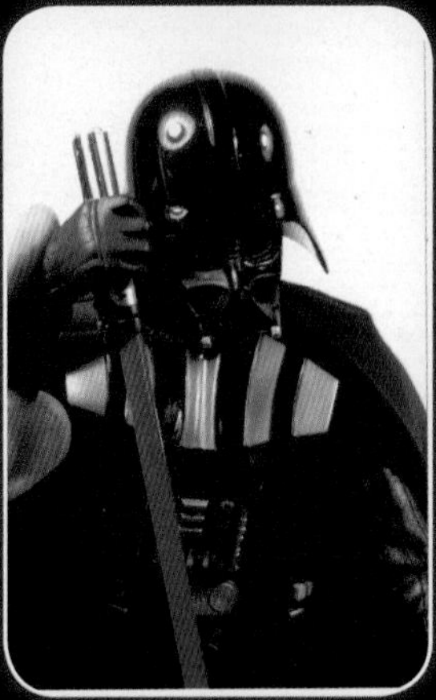

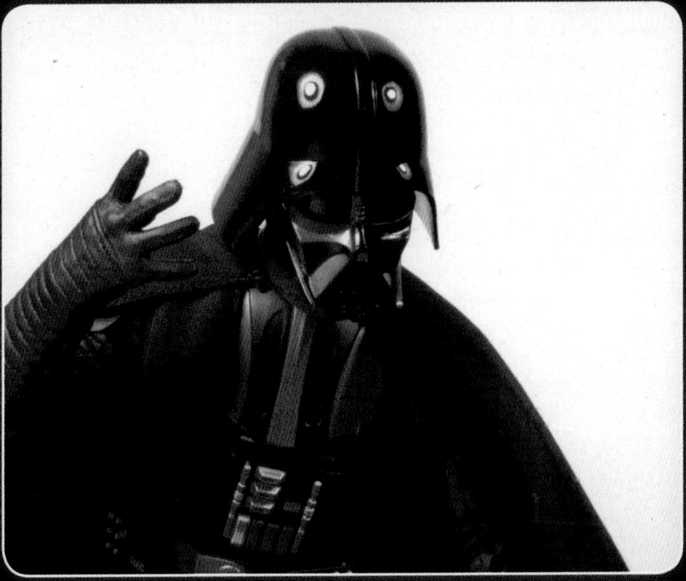

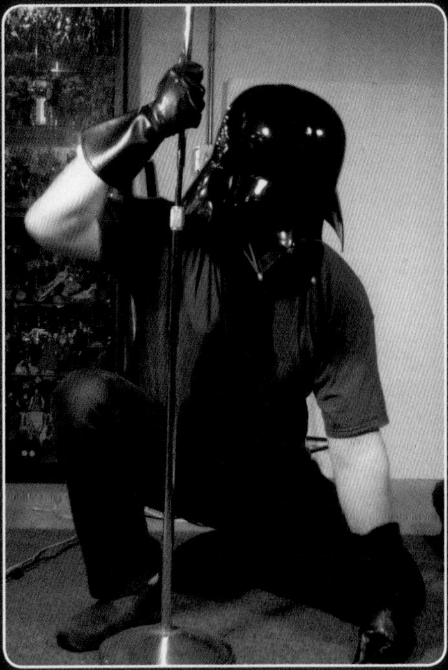

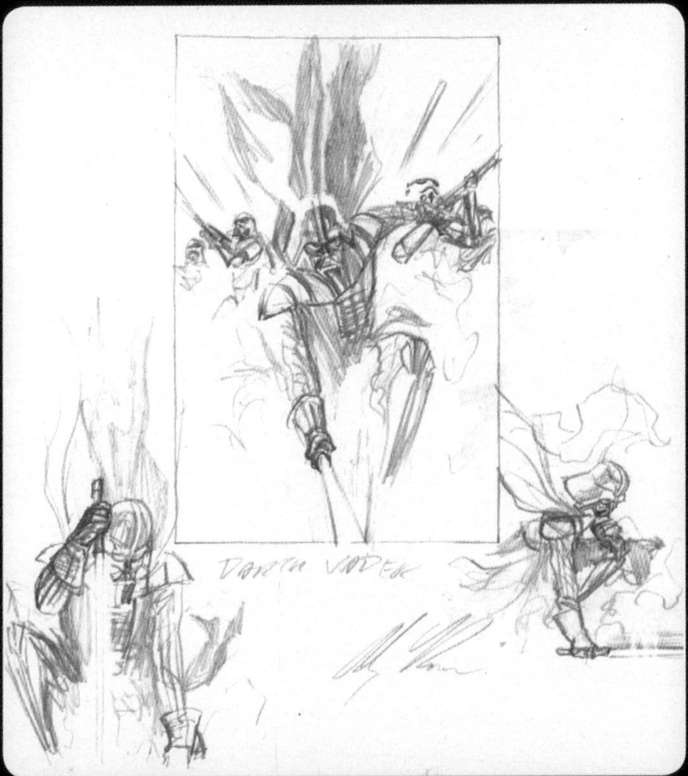
DARTH VADER

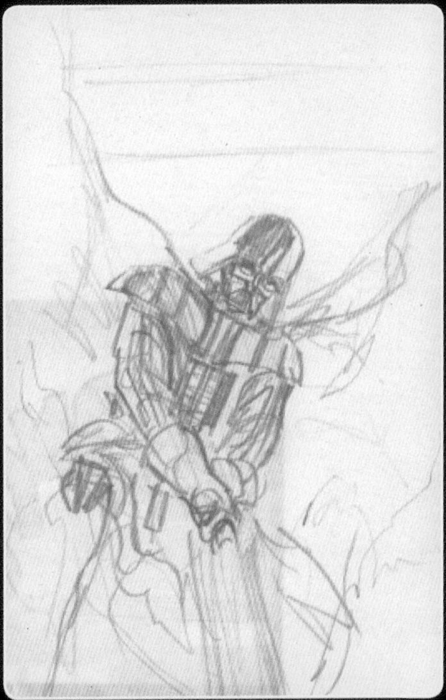

"For years I used to just enlarge my thumbnails by looking at them and re-drawing the compositions again. Often I found that I was disappointed in some aspect of figure drawing or all-over placements not matching what I had come to love in my thumbnails. I eventually took to photocopying these tight sketches, enlarging them to the twelve-by-eighteen-inches (or larger) size that I paint at. After a decade of carbon-tracing off the details, I now use a light box to do what everyone else had been doing for decades. This is why I can never use a computer, as my technical capabilities only advance to catch up to 20th-century standards.

"Upon tracing off my blown-up sketch at the full illustration size, I then draw from my printed photo reference. (Yes, I still print them.) I use their various details for guidance to hopefully make the piece look believable. I do not trace any part of the photos I take for my final drawing. My final art is an accurate or inaccurate interpretation of my photos drawn by simply looking at them.

"The pencils I use are usually a 4H to 7H hard lead to make a somewhat faint but sharp line that I can easily paint on top of and erase whatever might remain visible after. The paper I work on is a Strathmore Bristol Series 500 4 ply, vellum surface."

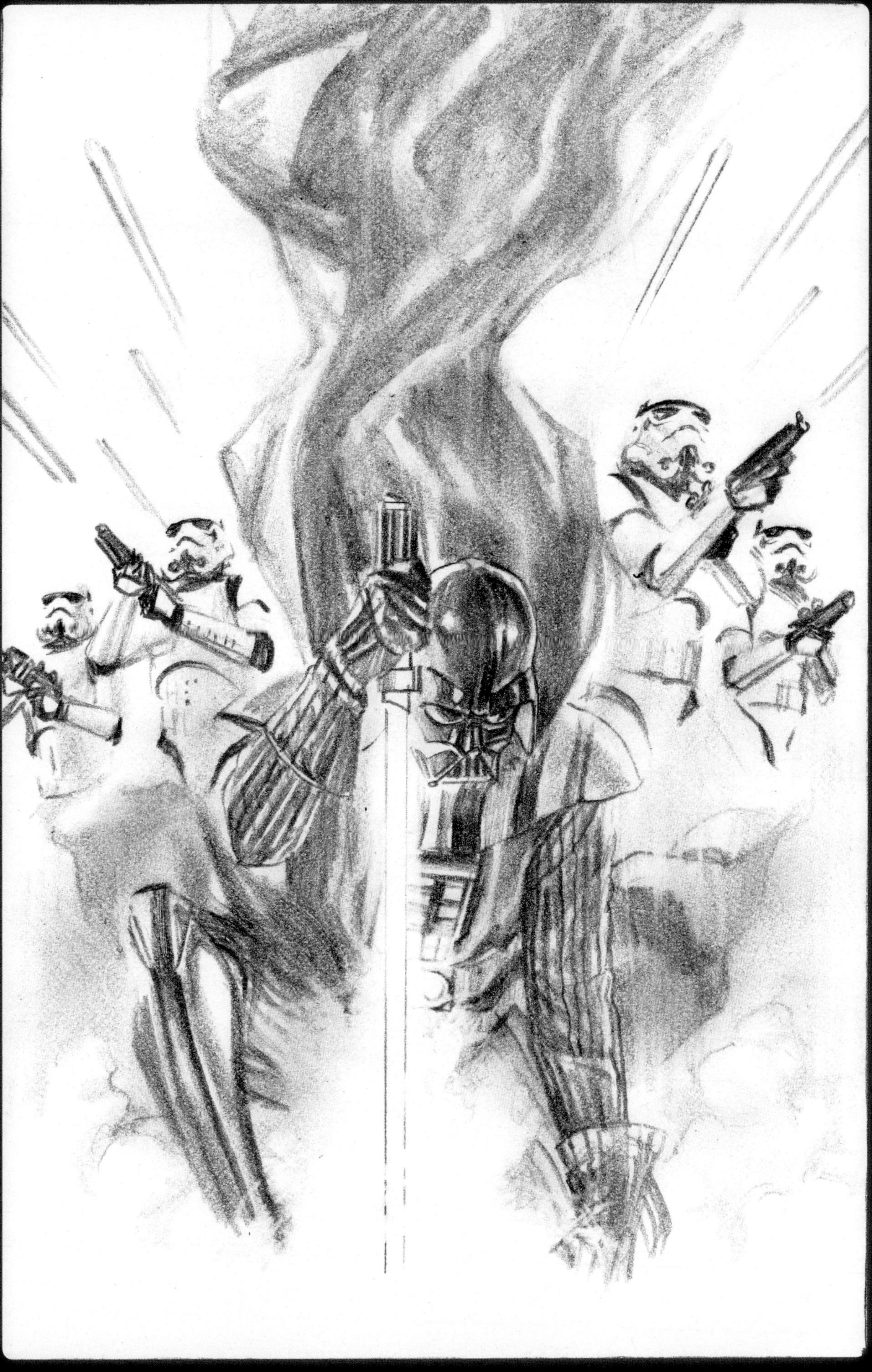

Darth Vader #1 Ross Sketch Variant—by Alex Ross

"For a long time, I've done an initial painting stage of black tonal watercolor/ gouache before building a full-color stage on top of that. I vary that approach more now based upon what lighting effect I might want the artwork to have. These days I will paint solid colors for certain areas before layering it with more detail and shading. In the case of the Vader cover, I only had two colors to use for this graphic approach. I painted a mid-tone-level gray with lamp black painted transparently. Usually I put in my deepest darks first with the black painted solidly, much like an inked illustration. I water the black down for the gradient half-tones throughout and do my best to avoid any splotchy absorption of the watercolor/gouache. For the one bit of color to have the smooth gradation that laser light demands, I used an airbrush to spray liquid acrylic paints. To preserve the bright light centers of the lightsaber and blaster lasers, I lay over a frisket film that sticks to the paper lightly, allowing me to cut around the area with an X-ACTO blade, leaving an exact shape that won't get hit by the airbrush. The airbrush is about as mechanical as I get in my overall process, and it's prone to spitting and other disasters.

"The final stage in this relatively easygoing piece was to imitate the spatter effect in the Tom Jung piece, which I did by using a solid watercolor/gouache white paint. I dip a brush in that paint and gently scrape it against the side of another brush, trying to carefully direct the direction of the dust/debris paint spatter."

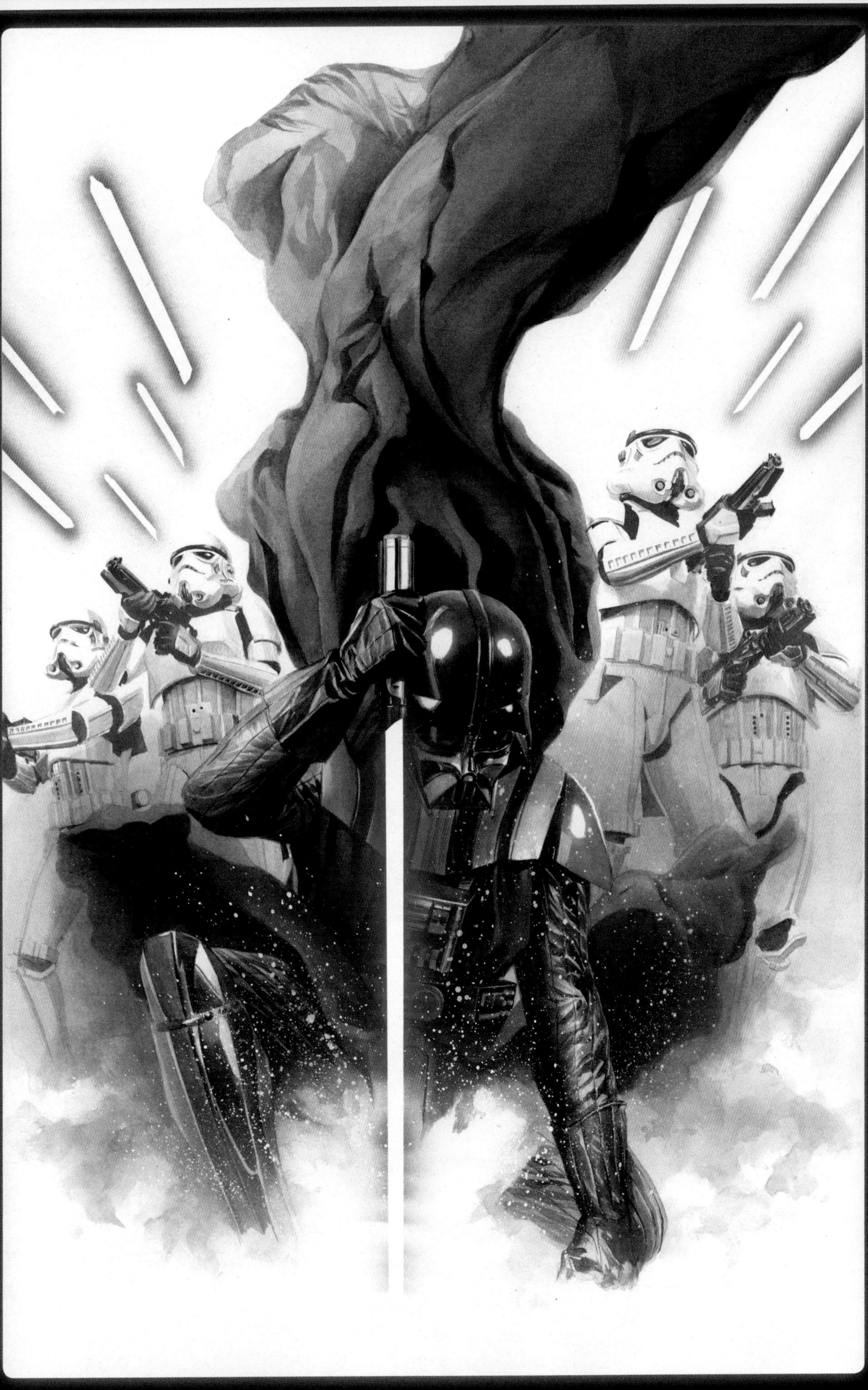

Darth Vader #1 Ross Variant—by Alex Ross

Darth Vader #1 Suayan Hastings Black and White Variant—by Mico Suayan

Darth Vader #1 Suayan Hastings Variant—pencils and inks by Mico Suayan, colors by Chris Sotomayor

Darth Vader #1 Young Variant—by Skottie Young

Darth Vader #2—by Adi Granov

Darth Vader #2 Dorman Classic Variant—by Dave Dorman

Darth Vader #2 Larroca Variant—pencils and inks by Salvador Larroca, colors by Edgar Delgado

Darth Vader #3—by Adi Granov

Darth Vader #3 Larroca Variant—pencils and inks by Salvador Larroca, colors by Edgar Delgado

Darth Vader #4—by Adi Granov

delgado

Darth Vader #4 Larroca Variant—pencils and inks by Salvador Larroca, colors by Edgar Delgado

Darth Vader #4 Noto Bam Variant—by Phil Noto

Darth Vader #5—by Adi Granov

Darth Vader #5 Larroca Variant—pencils and inks by Salvador Larroca, colors by Edgar Delgado

Darth Vader #6—by Adi Granov

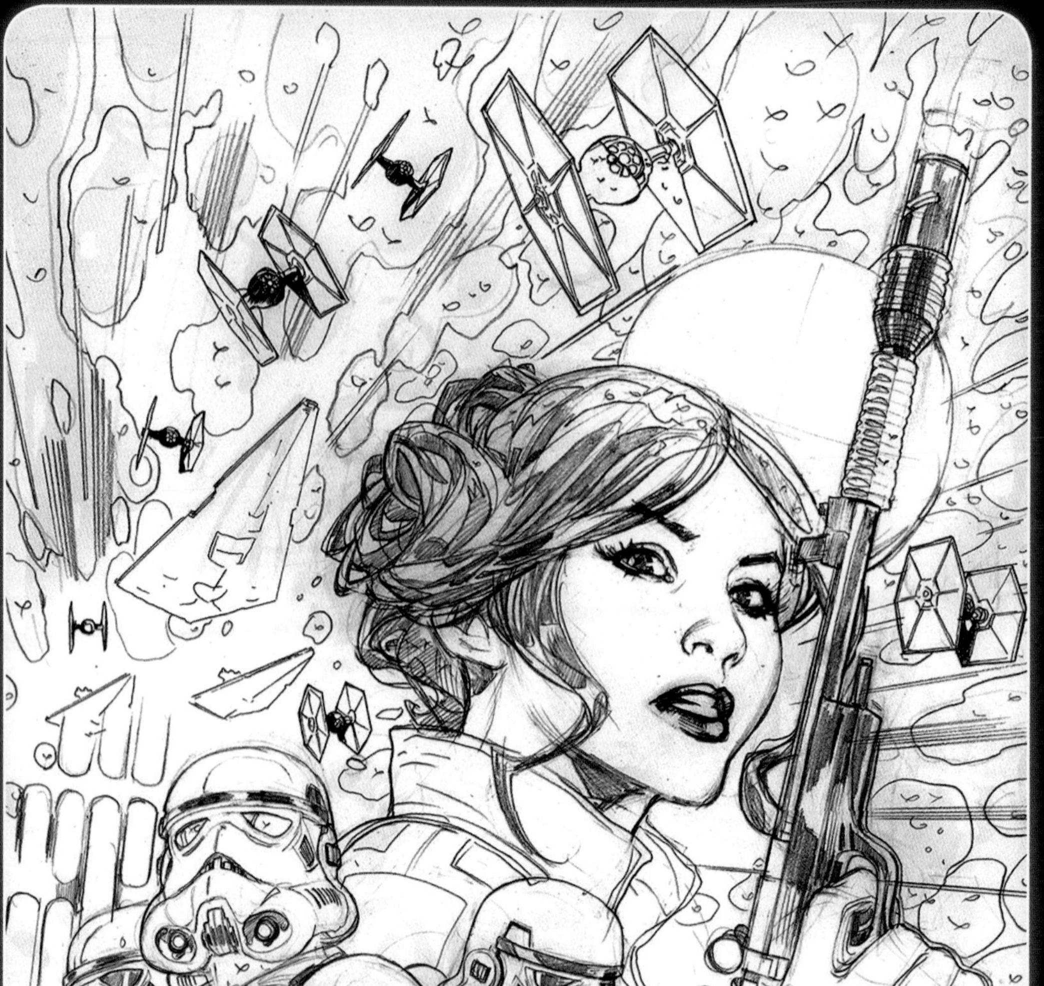

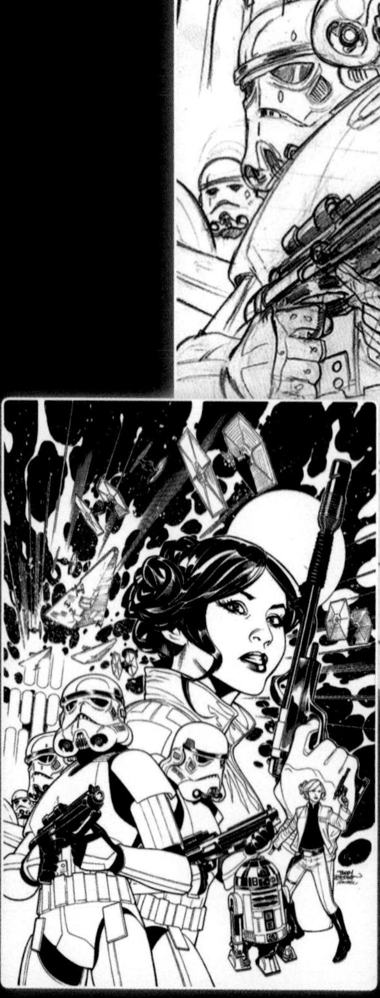

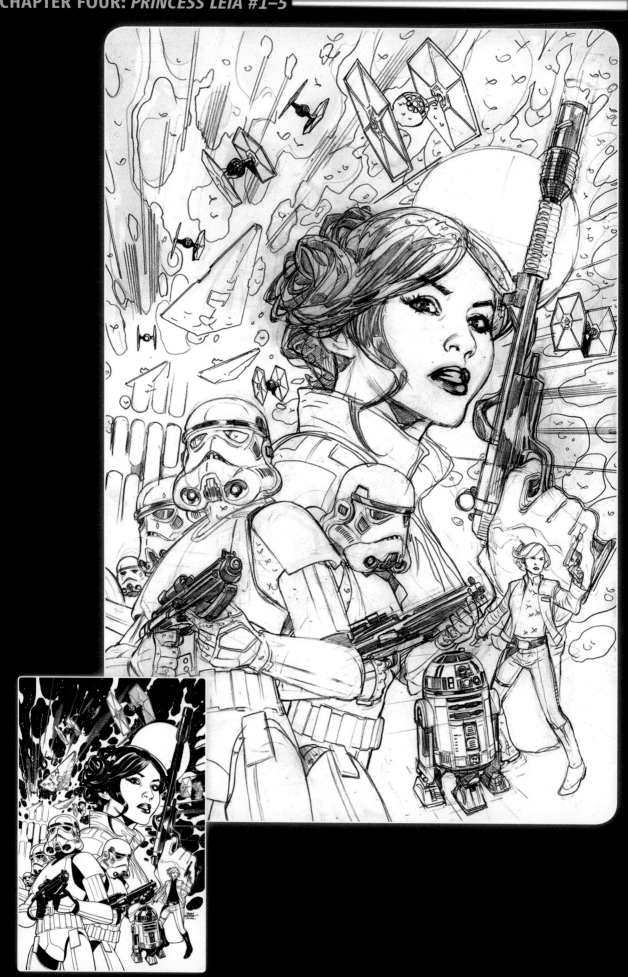

THERE IS ANOTHER...

Wars and *The Empire Strikes Back* are my two favorite films, so to set the comic between the two is awesome!"

And while seven-year old Dodson loved Chewbacca, the stormtroopers, and the Jawas most, his adult self has more traditional taste, choosing as his personal favorites Luke, Han, and—of course—Leia. Drawing her has only made Leia more fascinating to him: "Leia is someone in control or who takes control of a situation. It's great to see how she reacts when things don't go her way and how she overcomes that—and also, to explore what makes a person a princess, and how does that affect the choices you make."

...and that other, Princess Leia Organa of the doomed planet Alderaan, is every bit as heroic and brave as her brother, Luke Skywalker. Not that either twin is aware of their connection as the series *Princess Leia* begins. Picking right up in the Throne Room at the climax of *A New Hope*, writer Mark Waid sends Leia on a mission to rescue the scattered remains of her people before they fall prey to the Empire's deadly reprisals. Joining Waid on the series is Terry Dodson—an artist who, in tandem with wife and inker Rachel Dodson, has earned a reputation for depicting powerful women. As one of the leading figures in the Rebel Alliance, Leia certainly meets that description—and Dodson rates her as one of the finest in popular fiction. "Leia is definitely right up there in the pantheon," he says. "There's Leia, Ripley, Lara Croft, and Wonder Woman off the top of my head."

Dodson was seven years old when he first saw *A New Hope*, and it left a lifelong impression. "*Star Wars* is my favorite universe as a fan," he enthuses. "I'm a bigger fan of *Star Wars* than even Marvel super heroes. After seeing the movie, I bought everything *Star Wars*-related I could, including the Marvel comics—which were my first comic books—and that led me to reading comics regularly. *Star Wars* and comics then got me into drawing, so now it's all come full circle! I grew up on *Star Wars*, and the design of the universe is integral to my work no matter what I'm drawing. So to actually be working on a *Star Wars* comic, nothing could be more natural to me. And I couldn't have picked a better period to draw. When [Marvel Editor in Chief] Axel Alonso called to offer me the job, I almost did a backflip. *Star*

Illustrating an instantly recognizable pop-culture icon did not faze Dodson, a penciler who enjoys drawing likenesses and often bases aspects of his characters on real people. He describes likeness work as a great way to "test yourself as an artist," adding, "For something like *Star Wars*, I do try to develop a 'working likeness'—I figure out the gist of the likeness without being slavish to photographs. I try to make it feel like the character as opposed to feeling like a photograph. And in this case, it really helps to work on characters or actors you already like and where you know their personality." And when it comes to summing up that personality in one word, Dodson is decisive: "Attitude." He expands, "She does so many great expressions in *Star Wars* that I'm just trying to capture that."

In *Princess Leia #1*, proceedings begin with Leia in her ceremonial dress from the celebration scene, but she soon transitions into an outfit a little more suitable for adventuring. With *Star Wars* design sense part of his creative DNA, Dodson studied art books from the various movies to finalize her look, including what is perhaps Leia's most famous feature: her hair.

"I just studied everything available and assumed Alderaanian females will have what I'm going to call 19th-century Northern European styles. Leia's bun-do, her ceremonial do, her two looks in *Empire*—those all remind me of the hair in fashion in Europe in the later 19th century, so I based all her hairstyles on that. Men, I still stick with 1977 clean-cut England." Dodson had special assistance in the hair department, as his wife and inker went above and beyond the call of duty. "I had Rachel demonstrate with her hair how all these hairdos really work in the real world and how to style them. You can't make that stuff up! Well, men can, but there are female readers who will spot the errors miles away."

Joining Leia on her adventures is an original character, Evaan Verlaine, an Alderaanian pilot who pledges her loyalty to the princess. Dodson enjoyed adding a new face to the *Star Wars* universe. "Mark Waid said to make her Leia's opposite—tall, blonde, and light-eyed,"

Dodson says. "I added the chiseled cheekbones, the more slanted almond eyes, and thicker arched eyebrows. I then gave her that chignon hairdo and a similar type of thing for Leia—just a more relaxed version of Leia's hair for *Empire*. Her initial costume is straight up out of the original film—X-wing pilot! And then I gave her Luke's ceremonial outfit from *A New Hope*, as I figured that's the casual look for X-wing pilots, and I've always loved that outfit—especially Luke's yellow jacket—and loved having the chance to draw it." The artist enjoys the interplay of the two characters: the headstrong Leia and her would-be protector. "Leia is the princess—so I really try to play that," he says. "The funny thing is Leia is so much shorter than Evaan, so that's really fun to play with on the page."

But as Dodson continues to add to the *Star Wars* canon, as a self-confessed "huge fan" he feels a sense of responsibility to make sure that everything he draws honors what has come before. Whether it's a character, a vehicle, or a new world, Dodson is hardwired to make it fit in the galaxy he grew up with. Or as the penciler himself puts it, "When I design something, it's done with knowledge and respect of the films." That's exactly the kind of reverence and dedication to duty that would win the favor of a notoriously hard-to-impress princess.

Princess Leia #1—pencils and colors by Terry Dodson, inks by Rachel Dodson

Princess Leia #1 Brooks Midtown Comics Black and White Variant—by Mark Brooks

Princess Leia #1 Brooks Midtown Comics Variant—by Mark Brooks

Princess Leia #1 Brooks Variant—by Mark Brooks

Princess Leia #1 Campbell Connecting Variant—pencils and inks by J. Scott Campbell, colors by Nei Ruffino

"You're my only hope."

Princess Leia #1 Cassaday Teaser Variant—pencils and inks by John Cassaday, colors by Laura Martin

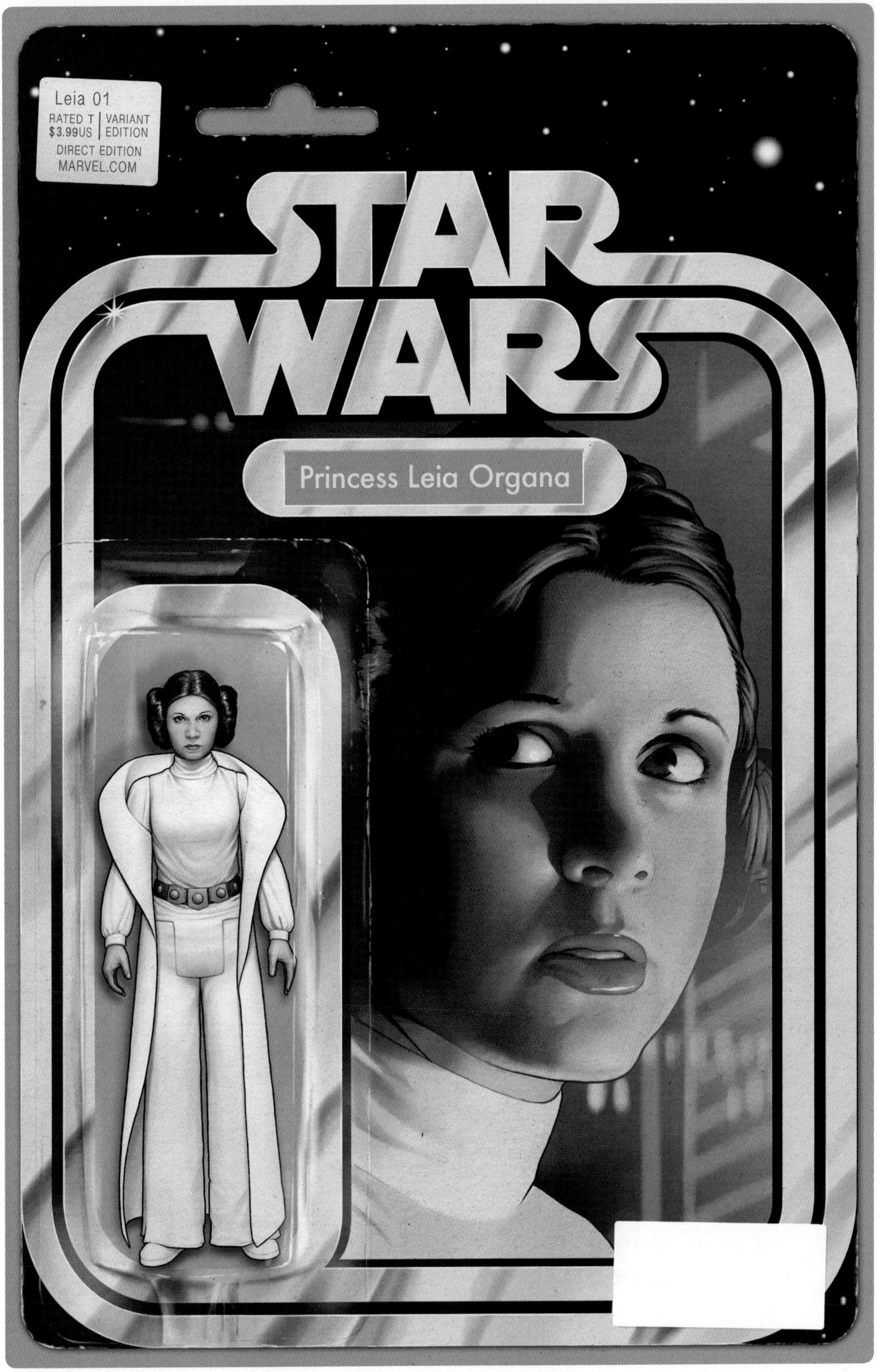
Leia 01
RATED T $3.99US
VARIANT EDITION
DIRECT EDITION
MARVEL.COM
STAR WARS
Princess Leia Organa

Princess Leia #1 Christopher Action Figure Variant—by John Tyler Christopher

Princess Leia #1 Conner Bam Black and White Variant—by Amanda Conner

Princess Leia #1 Conner Bam Variant—pencils and inks by Amanda Conner, colors by Edgar Delgado

Princess Leia #1 Movie Variant

Princess Leia #1 Dell'Otto Mile High Comics Variant—by Gabriele Dell'Otto

Princess Leia #1 Granov Emerald City Comicon Black and White Variant—by Adi Granov

Princess Leia #1 Granov Emerald City Comicon Variant—by Adi Granov

Princess Leia #1 Guice Classic Variant—pencils and inks by Jackson Guice, colors by Chris Sotomayor

Princess Leia #1 Horn GameStop Variant—by Greg Horn

Princess Leia #1 Land Dynamite Entertainment Variant—pencils and inks by Greg Land, colors by Justin Ponsor

Princess Leia #1 AlexRossStore.com Variant—by Alex Ross

Princess Leia #1 Ross Sketch Variant—by Alex Ross

Princess Leia #1 Ross Variant—by Alex Ross

Princess Leia #1 Suayan Hastings Black and White Variant—by Mico Suayan

Princess Leia #1 Suayan Hastings Variant—pencils and inks by Mico Suayan, colors by Chris Sotomayor

Princess Leia #1 Young Variant—by Skottie Young

Princess Leia #2—pencils and colors by Terry Dodson, inks by Rachel Dodson

Princess Leia #2 Dell'Otto Mile High Comics Variant—by Gabriele Dell'Otto

Princess Leia #2 Maleev Variant—by Alex Maleev

Princess Leia #3—pencils and colors by Terry Dodson, inks by Rachel Dodson

Princess Leia #3 Dell'Otto Mile High Comics Variant—by Gabriele Dell'Otto

Princess Leia #3 Francavilla Variant—by Francesco Francavilla

Princess Leia #3 Noto Bam Variant—by Phil Noto

Princess Leia #4—pencils and colors by Terry Dodson, inks by Rachel Dodson

Princess Leia #4 Dell'Otto Mile High Comics Variant—by Gabriele Dell'Otto

Princess Leia #5—pencils and colors by Terry Dodson, inks by Rachel Dodson

Princess Leia #5 Dell'Otto Mile High Comics Variant—by Gabriele Dell'Otto

A LONG TIME AGO...

...in the summer of 1977, thousands of comics fans got their first glimpse of Luke Skywalker—on the cover of Marvel's original *Star Wars #1*. Released weeks before *Star Wars* Episode IV *A New Hope* would transform cinema forever, the eye-catching comic book boldly asked of Luke: "Will he save the galaxy—or destroy it?" The book presented the initial answer to eager readers over a six-issue adaptation of the first film, before continuing the saga for nine years—through *The Empire Strikes Back* to *Return of the Jedi* and beyond.

Across 107 issues of the main series, three annuals and the four-issue *Star Wars: Return of the Jedi* limited series, Marvel expanded the *Star Wars* universe, taking the beloved band of rebels on uncanny adventures with friends and foes both familiar and new. In addition to the rabbit-faced Jaxxon, Luke, Han, Leia, and the rest encountered the space pirate Crimson Jack, the roguish smuggler Rik Duel, and the telepathic race known as the Hoojibs—not to mention an oddly walrus-like Jabba the Hut (with only one "t") that predated the corpulent character's more familiar on-screen design. But the series still had plenty of room for further clashes with fan favorites like Boba Fett and—of course—Darth Vader.

And it was all courtesy of some of the comic-book industry's finest talents of the time—not least the legendary Roy Thomas, whose own perseverance brought the project to Marvel. Working directly with George Lucas, Thomas guided the book through its first year as writer and editor. He was joined by artist Howard Chaykin, whose dynamic style proved ideal for translating the cinematic space opera to the printed page. In subsequent years, a suitably stellar roster of creators lent their talents to the title—including Archie Goodwin, Chris Claremont, J.M. DeMatteis, David Michelinie, Carmine Infantino, and Walter Simonson.

For painter Alex Ross—who paid wonderful tribute to the classic series with his two *Star Wars #1* variants, homaging both the original first-issue cover and its fondly remembered Luke Skywalker corner box—the original adaptation served as his introduction to *Star Wars*, when the first three issues were collected in a tabloid-size Special Edition in the summer of 1977. For the wide-eyed, seven-year-old Ross, Chaykin's art in that format fueled his excitement to see the film. "The interpretation in comic-book art of the film's details teased what was there, but really created a longing for

seeing the picture more," he says. "When Al Williamson stepped up to do the adaptations of the second and third films, his incredibly detailed, accurate representations created my enthusiasm for the comics."

Now, every issue of the classic Marvel *Star Wars* run has been collected in three wampa-sized Omnibus volumes; the adaptations of the original trilogy have also been remastered, recolored, and re-presented in a trio of stunning graphic novels, featuring new covers by Adi Granov. The artist describes it as a privilege and a career highlight to be asked to produce single images encapsulating the three films—a task that, dauntingly, would involve following in the giant footsteps of Drew Struzan, who played a key role in establishing the visual iconography of *Star Wars* in his unforgettable film posters for the series. "I am a really big fan of Drew Struzan, and he has had a big influence on me throughout my career," Granov says. "Having said that, in my work I try to present a bit more of a stylized, comic-book dynamic, deviating from photorealistic images from the film. I attempted to combine some of the Struzan approach with the collages of characters, but with a more comic-book type of layout with more heroic figures as the central focus. I felt that was more appropriate to the comic covers, as well as more honest to my own sensibilities."

While he didn't strive for photorealism, Granov recognized the importance of capturing the spirit of characters so ingrained in the public consciousness. "Likenesses are a very interesting aspect of the work, but they are almost like a cheat since it's the easiest way to impress the readers, as they have something to immediately hook onto," he says. "But a poor likeness can really ruin an otherwise good image, so it's very important to get it right. I find it pretty easy if they are bigger on the page, but quite difficult if the face on the drawing is as small as my thumbnail. This was a particular challenge on the *A New Hope* and *Return of the Jedi* covers."

In this chapter, we present Granov's graphic-novel covers alongside those produced for the Omnibus volumes, including direct-market variants by Greg Hildebrandt. But first, to celebrate the wonderful legacy of the original series, savor a gallery of some of its finest covers—images that capture all the action, adventure, and fun of *Star Wars* in the Mighty Marvel Manner!

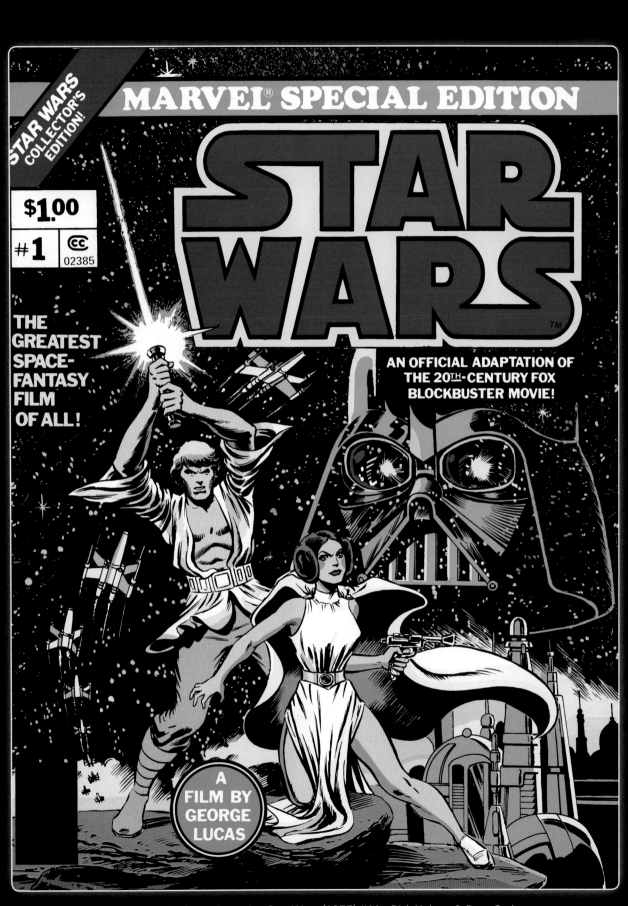

Marvel Special Edition Featuring Star Wars (1977) #1 by Rick Hoberg & Dave Cockrum

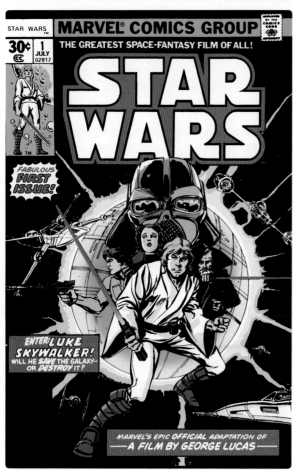

Star Wars (1977) #1 by Howard Chaykin

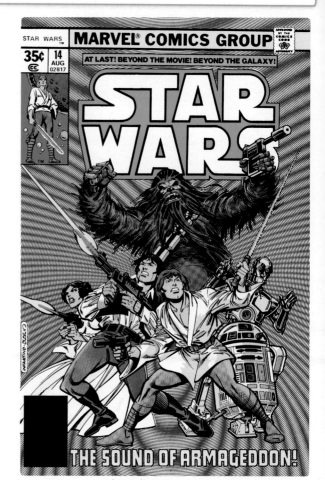

Star Wars (1977) #14 by Carmine Infantino

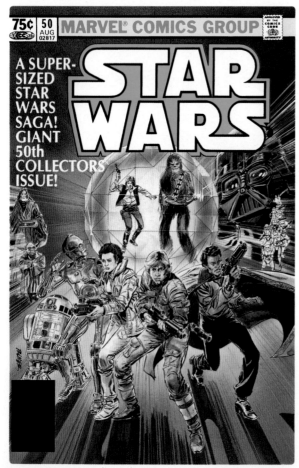

Star Wars (1977) #50 by Walter Simonson

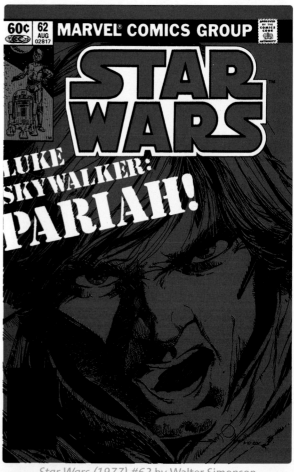

Star Wars (1977) #62 by Walter Simonson

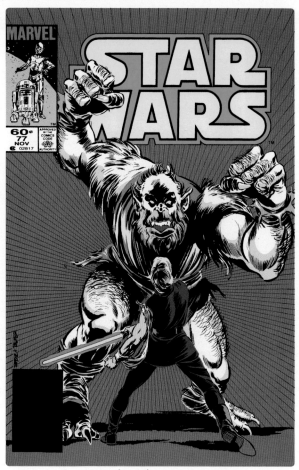

Star Wars (1977) #77 by Ron Frenz

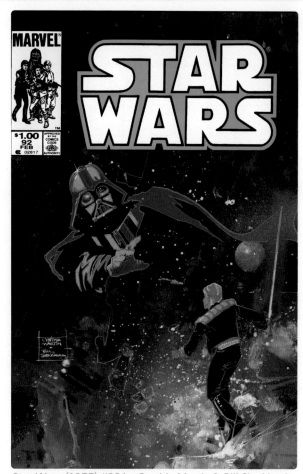

Star Wars (1977) #92 by Cynthia Martin & Bill Sienkiewicz

Star Wars (1977) #94 by Cynthia Martin

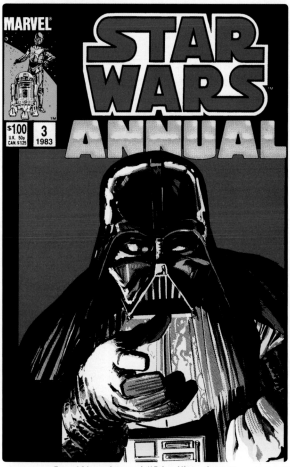

Star Wars Annual #3 by Klaus Janson

213

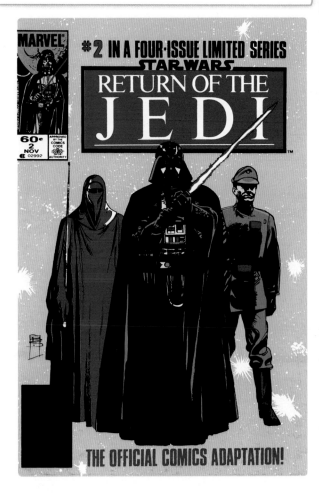

Star Wars: Return of the Jedi #1–4 by Bill Sienkiewicz

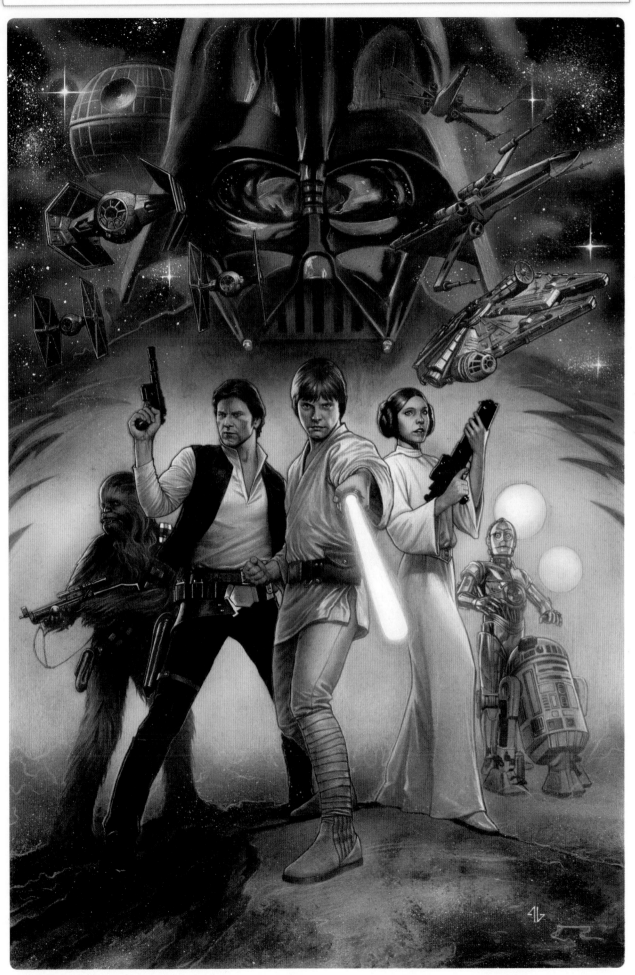

Star Wars Episode IV *A New Hope* by Adi Granov

Star Wars Episode V *The Empire Strikes Back* by Adi Granov

Star Wars Episode VI *Return of the Jedi* by Adi Granov

Star Wars: The Original Marvel Years Omnibus Vol. 1 by Howard Chaykin, colors by Edgar Delgado

Star Wars: The Original Marvel Years Omnibus Vol. 1 Variant by Greg Hildebrandt

Star Wars: The Original Marvel Years Omnibus Vol. 2 by Gene Day, colors by Edgar Delgado

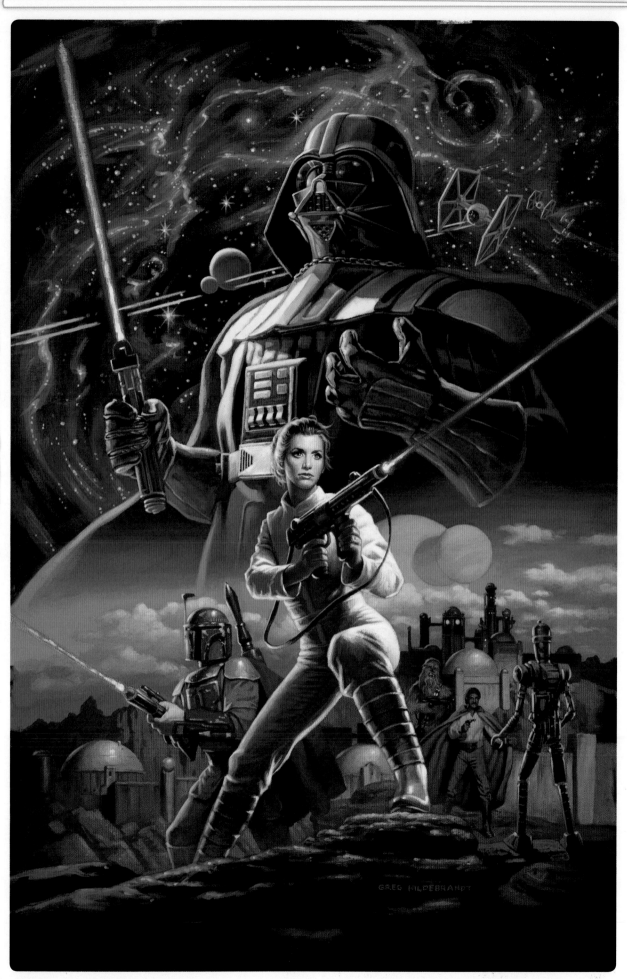

Star Wars: The Original Marvel Years Omnibus Vol. 2 Variant by Greg Hildebrandt

Star Wars: The Original Marvel Years Omnibus Vol. 3 by Tom Palmer

Star Wars: The Original Marvel Years Omnibus Vol. 3 Variant by Greg Hildebrandt